MW00974016

CAUGHT IN THE RIP

CAUGHT IN THE RIP

CUTTING ACROSS THE CONVENTIONAL WISDOM TO MAKE WISE DECISIONS

Dear Chris + Christina

Perhaps this will
help on the next
stage of your journey!

Every best John

JOHN A THOMPSON

Published by
Beechwood International Ltd
51 Queen Anne St
London W1G 9HS

Website: www.caughtintherip.com
Email enquiries and orders to citr@beechwood.net

First published in Great Britain in 2005
© John A Thompson 2005

The right of John A Thompson to be identified as the author of this work
has been asserted by him in accordance with the Copyright, Designs and
Patents Act 1988.

British Library Cataloguing in Publication Data
A CIP catalogue record for this book is available from the British Library

ISBN 0-9551212-0-5

Edited by Edwina Thompson
Cover design by Scott Hopkin
Text design and typesetting by Studio Pazzo, Melbourne

Printed in China at Everbest Printing Co Ltd

To my father,
with gratitude for
his practical wisdom
and sense of humour

CONTENTS

PREFACE

What is this book about?

Etched in my Australian childhood memory is a terrifying experience in the Sydney surf. Oblivious to the hidden danger of a smooth sea, I suddenly realised that I had been swept beyond my depth, a long way from the shore. I was caught in a rip. After finding my bearings, with youthful invincibility I began to swim back toward the beach. But no matter how hard I struggled, the shore continued to recede. Fortunately I discovered my plight before it was too late, and found that swimming across the current was the only way out.

This book aims to make sense of our battles with the similarly treacherous undertow of life's journey, as we try to make *wise* decisions in both our career and personal relationships. You will see that it does not aim to espouse another neat process for effective decision-making *per se*; there are plenty of expert textbooks and training programmes already available on that subject. Instead, the book addresses some of the hard questions at the root of our decision-making.

It started early last year, when I planned to take a month out to jot down any wisdom I may have gained through my attempts to buck the system. You probably need to know that I like to see myself as a bit of a radical, constantly tempted by the idea that 'if it's not broken, break it and put it back together again', and that

1

I continue to urge many other like-spirits to overcome their fear and challenge 'the way we do things around here'. There is a downside of course; my wife accuses me of being a malcontent, so 37 years of marriage says much for her endurance.

I abruptly resigned from one of my first jobs after daring to question Big Ed, my Texan boss who loomed large in every way. A traditionalist prior to the advent of 'political correctness', he got away with saying that he had a mind to take me down the back of the woodshed for a good whipping. I was a slow learner. Later, after a short time in the UK, an old-school English boss diplomatically suggested it might be better for everyone if I returned to the colony where I belong.

Notably, I was never threatened with the sack, saved only by a few runs on the scoreboard and support from those around me. My lack of judgement was probably more to do with the manner in which I raised the difficult questions, so in later years I have focused on sharing some hard-earned lessons with the next generation of movers and shakers.

After a gruelling eighteen months of obsession, this little volume has finally emerged to explore three key challenges in the quest to make wise decisions. The first confronts the overpowering ebbs and flow of conventional wisdom, and helps to identify and reassess important working assumptions upon which we rely in our everyday lives. This leads to the second challenge, which deals with the way we think and engage with others. The third challenge tackles the practical implications of questioning entrenched opinions and having the guts to do things differently.

'The conventional wisdom' is a phrase introduced to the English language by eminent economist John Kenneth Galbraith, and wryly described by London *Financial Times* columnist John Kay as 'opinions that, while not necessarily well founded, are so widely held among the rich and influential that only the rash and foolish will endanger their careers by dissenting from them'. Most people agree that much of our baggage is received wisdom, adopted uncritically as we rush through life. The 'uninquiring mind', according to Kay, is what's needed for the development of the conventional wisdom, which is:

> ... more common than ever today in business, in finance, in politics; in individuals who gain comfort from every cliché about the universality of globalisation, the transforming influence of information technology and the historic inevitability of liberal and active capital markets. But the academic or the lawyer is bound to ask questions such as 'what does he actually think?' or even 'what is true?'

Why, though, should we leave it to the academics and lawyers to ask the hard questions? In your busy life, how frequently do you probe the prevailing view, deliberately asking questions rather than making statements? What's more, how often do you go out of your way to encourage others to question you, in the hope that you might then see and do things in a different way?

Perhaps you have decided it's not worth the aggravation, or feel similarly to Sir Winston Churchill who famously admitted: 'I am always ready to learn, but I do not always like being taught.' Some pretend they are open to challenge, but as Kay parodies, statements such as, 'we would really like you to challenge our ideas', should be treated in the same spirit as 'tell me honestly what you think of my new dress'. This certainly rings true for me. Often the most articulate and apparently confident business leaders, when challenged on the run, appear confused regarding the basis of their thinking. They are quick to take umbrage, and yet impatiently complain 'if only they understood me better'.

On looking back, clearly I too am guilty of being caught up in the cut and thrust of practical living, often at the expense of pursuing the deeper issues. So what are these hard questions, and to whom do we turn for answers, both in the present and from the past? I have tried to glean a sense of the various pathways taken through history by some of the great philosophers, theologians and scientists, primarily via the short cut of analyses by those who have made such study their life's work. This is also expedient because my cognitive skills are not in the same league as an Aristotle, Descartes, Hume or Kant.

I have cited a range of people with very different views, some widely recognised and others not so. Of course there is also much to learn by carefully observing the ups and downs of ordinary lives encountered every day. To the people who have knowingly or unknowingly helped me on my way, thank you. It is encouraging to remember the old axiom that some of the greatest heroes are unknown and unsung, unaware of their own significance.

Who should read this book?

This book is for anyone who is perplexed by the state of the Western world, seriously thinks about why this is so, and would like to do something about it. My main concern is for those people in their twenties and thirties, who will make decisions that shape the future. They may be budding lawyers, doctors, counsellors, politicians, teachers, NGO workers, clergy, academics, entrepreneurs, writers, film producers, consultants, or managers in business.

Picture, for example, an ambitious and influential young couple, both gym-fit, well educated and informed, enjoying business or professional careers. They have done very well and the future is full of promise and goals. They might even have one or two great little kids and try to share the load equally; or more commonly, one stays at home to juggle the domestic demands with a continuing part time job. The other is a young manager who must deliver unrealistic targets, motivate a number of colleagues and participate in a wider team, often global, which requires a combination of travel and regular teleconferences at any time of the day or night. Heady and demanding stuff.

However, there is more to the picture for these loosely labelled Generation Xers, who have been led to believe by their baby boomer parents (dubbed Generation R for rest, recreation, and now recycled retirees) that they can have it all. Even though their combined pay package is pretty impressive, they still struggle to balance the budget, and fight perpetual tiredness.

They also struggle to make sense of a divided and battered world, because they have *a strong sense of social justice, a strong sense of 'right' and 'wrong', and aim to give their children a strong foundation for their lives.* Around them they see families fracturing and kids wilting under pressure. They experience harsh corporate initiatives shrugged off as 'commercial realities'. They don't trust their politicians or the media. They watch 'decent' young people from 'decent' families inflict unimaginable humiliation on others, in their own army barracks and far-flung places like Abu Ghraib; and they know only the intrusive power of television and courageous reporting prevent these images from being suppressed or spun.

They might support a charity, and are most definitely moved to respond generously to appeals for help in tragedies of the scale of the Asian tsunami. Yet they vote for tax cuts and increased expenditure on services, even though their government allocates a paltry amount for foreign aid, the starving, and the marginalised, and drags out the misery of refugees with no place to go.

Soothed by drive-time radio after another hard day, they might also tune in to debates about the economic, social, political and ethical questions of the moment. When they hear about the latest corporate scandal, they contemplate why apparently intelligent and principled people can act corruptly whilst at the helm of important enterprises. And as they idle in the traffic, burning petrol, it is disconcerting for them to hear about the devastating effects of global warming.

On the weekend they indulge in some well-earned retail therapy, nudge the plastic again, throw another steak on the barbie, down a cold beer with their mates, and bemoan the state of politics, the media, management, customer service, security queues and the traffic. When shocking statistics, news stories and movies overwhelm, they either shake their heads or shout, knowing they cannot be heard above the noise.

But they don't muck around; life must go on. They continually make decisions under pressure, the quality depending on their ability to identify the most viable options and choose 'the best one'. When it comes to religion, they may have some vague past experience, good or bad, but have long since discarded it as being of any practical use. Some of their friends may be experimenting with 'alternative' spiritual or philosophical ideas.

Is this profile comparable with yours, or others you care for and know well? If it is, this little family unit is one of the most crucial pillars of our society today, and will be even more so for the future. Whilst tapping away on the keyboard, you have been uppermost in my mind.

I am particularly conscious of our 'son-and-heir' Scott and his wife Kate, as they decide how to equip their two babies, Oliver and Emily, to make wise choices. In fact, this book is written to our three adult children (I refer to Prue and Edwina later – they straddle the Generation X and Y divide), living in a contemporary urban world and each of whom my wife and I are intensely proud. Hopefully some of the lessons arising from my predecessors and personal experience may help them make better decisions in their professional and personal lives, by anticipating a few of the inevitable pitfalls ahead.

I also hope they find the ideas sufficiently worthy to share with their offspring and friends, and it will be a bonus if anyone else takes the time to read it (especially if you are someone who has wondered whether there is any coherent thinking behind my apparently piecemeal contributions to *ad hoc* debates across the dinner table, and elsewhere).

Why should you bother to read on?

In a world of information overload, I have no reputation as an author and suspect this will be my first and last attempt at writing about something of fundamental importance. Perhaps it might appeal simply because I am not some expert, well-known figure espousing his view of life, but a mere bit player further down the journey who, like you, had limited time, resources and ability to devote to the big questions. It might appeal because I know a number in your peer group very well, both through business and family, and they know me, warts and all. In fact, to expose my thinking so transparently after all these years is somewhat like stripping naked in Oxford Street during London's sales.

Hopefully it will appeal because of my genuine intent primarily to model a suggested process for clear thinking and to demonstrate the importance of putting the right kind of questions to the right kind of people, rather than just putting my views. I am very mindful that libraries have been filled over the centuries on every subject addressed. You will also see that I draw heavily on my lifetime experience in the field of business because of its influence on the way many people think and act today.

Whether you are in business or not, the following scenario probably strikes a chord. In 1972 I opened an account at one of Britain's oldest high street banks, where I soon discovered that the customer came a poor third to shareholders and staff. In 2005 my experience is not noticeably any better, although strangely the profits still pour in to the coffers. The queue is the same length, and with the odd notable exception, tellers are still behind a barrier, looking like they wished it were Friday. I even used to enjoy the support of a concerned bank manager; now I have a different chirpy 'relationship manager' every few months, contactable only through a call centre. This lack of discernible improvement is despite the huge effort and expenditure I know this bank has invested in motivating staff to improve their 'customer relationships'.

A friend of mine is about to complete a business book on managing relationships, which he considers to be the fundamental challenge for contemporary managers who want to make wise decisions. Like the word 'challenge', it is not surprising that 'relationships' is another defining word of our age. When embarking on a new project, it is sobering to realise just how many relationships are crucial to success. The same applies at the personal level; for example, by introducing another child to a family of four, the existing six relationships, which are not always perfect, are increased by two thirds.

I have expended much energy as a manager and business consultant facilitating teams and organisations to lift their game by getting people 'onto the same page'. To decide the agenda for action, various constituencies or 'stakeholders' first have to agree where they are today as a business and a culture. Two points are used to assess this place on the road map: where they have come from and where they want to be in the longer term. With sufficient resolve, we usually reach agreement on business goals, strategies, and the behaviours required to implement the plans and so deliver the objectives.

When participants then resume the journey and encounter practical obstacles that derail their plans, two things can happen. First, they argue about which is the more meaningful benchmark to assess performance (and bonuses) – sometimes characterised as the real versus the wishful. For example, typically the workers refer to the previous 'actual figures' and the bosses refer to 'the budget'; or if it suits their case, either party may blame external factors beyond their control!

Secondly, they realise that it is futile to attempt to change any obstacle that is the effect of a deeper cause. So they dig down, and usually discover that there is a 'cause and effect chain', where each cause in turn becomes the symptom of a deeper cause. In the process they may get down to the drivers of behaviour, i.e. personal values, but people rarely take the final plunge to address the *origin* of their values. *I suspect unrecognised clashes at this level may be the deep-seated cause of many collapses in even the best-laid plans.*

In my work I have never been given a mandate to dig this deeply. Understandably, some shy away from this issue because they believe it is too hard to figure out; and if it is hard for the individual, it becomes progressively more difficult for couples, teams, organisations, communities and nations. Some fear that we will open a can of worms that might lead to painful division; the basic frameworks driving individuals are at least diverse and often contradictory and flimsy, yet firmly held. Many consider it to be their private domain, best left well alone. Nevertheless, these are probably reasons why the plaintive cry, 'I need to know where you are coming from', constantly echoes down thousands of corridors and telephone cables, and reverberates in the minds of combatants at home.

I readily confess there have been times when my zeal to understand another's position has been perceived as intrusive and offensive, with the lesson that every encounter can teach us more about how to engage with others in a meaningful and constructive manner. Someone once said that if you throw mud, not only do you get your hands dirty, you also lose a lot of ground. One of my favourite passions is a particular Aussie Rules football team, and apparently it is amusing to watch me in earnest discussion with a great mate who supports a deadly rival. As long as our focus is on the respective *clubs*, ne'er the twain shall meet (and it doesn't help when my opponent is a foot taller). Here the lesson is simple: what binds us is our shared zeal for the *code*.

The state of our complex interactions with each other, and the environment, is why we have made a mess of things that appear intrinsically beautiful and good. There are people trying to repair some of the damage done, but frequently they work at cross-purposes, because of different motivations and vested interests. When observing two neighbours abusing each other across the street, famous eighteenth century English wit, Sydney Smith, commented: 'those two will never agree, they are arguing from different premises.'

A key pre-requisite for rational, consistent decision-making, at work and in our personal relationships, is an *agreed* reference framework, or a *fixed* set of standards against which we can mutually interrogate our options. This is the glue essential for effective co-existence and collaboration.

What is more, without a common code, belief system, cause or identity, a vacuum exists, and vacuums demand to be filled. There is much competition for this hungry space, from the most strident activists, to the more subtle influences that pervade our society. How much does our personal identity rely on our football team, whom we work for, our religion, the school we select for our kids, where we live or go for holidays, and the brands we buy? Advertising strategists even espouse the mantra *I shop therefore I am*. Then there is the effect of our cultural roots. Over the past sixteen years of my life in London, hardly a day has passed when my Australianness has worked either for or against me!

Many argue that no diverse civilisation can function without a common 'worldview', or unifying system of thought. Anthropologist David Burnett explains that worldviews strongly influence cultures, by filtering and organising experiences and information that come to us each day. He also says that the ideas and values of a particular worldview, or conventional wisdom if you like, seem to be self-evidently true to its adherents.

This leads us to the age-old question, made ever more pertinent in our modern world where we claim to value diversity: can people objectively find some ultimate point of convergence, against which to resolve differences and achieve unity? Is there, as some declare, an elusive 'integral' worldview? Contrary to post-modernist thought, I believe we can only hope to achieve genuine harmony and sustainable results if we dare peel the onion to its core.

The skilled navigator will tell you that any set of position co-ordinates needs a fixed reference equivalent to true north. In life's journey the ultimate co-ordinates are those for our *origin* and *destiny*. If we are not clear about where we come from and where we are headed, how can we determine where we are and make wise decisions about where to go next? We will consciously or subconsciously make *ad hoc* decisions on the run, with the resultant inconsistency and injustice that trouble us and baffle others. I do hope this book encourages you to face these core questions head on.

How should you read this book?

I urge you to read this mini-journey of words with a helicopter view so that you can consider the argument in its entirety and avoid pre-emptive judgements. Crucial as they may appear to be, I recommend that you mark your questions about the detail as you go, and return to them later; you may just find that they assume less and less significance as the reasoning unfolds.

Any self-respecting advocate of modern management practices would feature the word 'process' early on, and volunteer some accompanying pearls of wisdom, otherwise known as commonsense. As you board the helicopter, here are mine in a nutshell: challenging the conventional wisdom requires a process of clear thinking and effective engagement with others, which highlights the need for simplicity, mutual understanding, and constructive dialogue.

I have tried to abide by the KISS principle – 'keep it simple stupid'. This does not imply that the quest for simplicity is effortless. In contrast to the easy option of being simplistic, it is a long and arduous journey. The well worn journey metaphor indicates that, when we arrive at our next 'there', it becomes our new 'here', making thinking and doing a step-by-step process of discovery, viewed by the optimist as an opportunity to learn and grow. And not just on the back of our 'successes'; those who make a real difference treat the tough times as gifts, because therein lies the opportunity to glean enduring wisdom.

To those with a vested interest in keeping it complicated (you might just be a lawyer or a management consultant), I quote the words of jazz musician Charlie Mingus:

> Anyone can play weird, that's easy.
> What's hard is to play as simple as Bach.
> Making the simple complicated is commonplace.
> Making the complicated simple, that's creativity.

Far from keeping it simple, in the twenty first century we in the West are faced with numerous and contradictory schools of thought, from all the hues of secularism to the kaleidoscope of Eastern and New Age spirituality, and warring factions within the church. This bewildering variety of options tends to complicate rather than bring order and sense to our lives. Although choice is good for economic progress, according to psychologist Barry Schwartz in his recent book, *The Paradox of Choice*, too much leaves us bemused and unhappy.

Over the centuries, we have been inundated with brilliant thinkers, but even they get confused and risk missing the forest for the trees. Cambridge Professor of Philosophy, Simon Blackburn, says at the end of his book *Think*:

> The harmony between our thoughts and the world, the bridge we build between past and future, the sense of what the physical world contains and how our minds fit into it, are all topics on which the finest thinkers have hurled themselves, only to be frustrated. There always seem to be better words, if only we could find them, just over the horizon.

Attempting to lift the reader from a state of pessimism, Blackburn finishes with an optimistic view of the abundance of ideas in the world and their value. But the degree of mutual understanding is inversely proportional to the number and range of ideas.

To help you understand my train of thought, this book is divided into three parts, each comprising three chapters. There is a schematic at the start of each part which highlights our progress. Chapters in the first two parts begin with an overview to help those who may like to skip the detail for topics of less concern to them.

At the beginning of our journey, Part I evaluates how conventional wisdom informs our decision-making in a dysfunctional world. It addresses key questions at a practical and philosophical level. If we are rocketing toward a major crossroad, with flashing lights signalling 'system failure', should we floor the accelerator even harder, or pause for a radical re-think about whether there is more to life than this? In the search for clues we look first within ourselves and then explore cutting edge science.

Indicators that there may be 'something beyond' our understanding of the here and now lead us into the theological field in Part II. You may be surprised to see how the need for justice emerges as humanity's most profound predicament.

We then cut to the chase in Part III, by exploring some potential implications for how we might have to change the way we think and behave, as we make decisions in both our professional and personal lives.

There are suggested exits at certain levels, which point to alternative pathways or worldviews chosen by many. If any of these different tracks appeal, you may care to progress your own thinking in that direction, and compare outcomes with those of this book. Remember, though, proponents of differing views will only have a constructive dialogue if they first agree on the prerequisite spirit and rules of engagement.

A good dose of old-fashioned *humility* is usually required to concede that we might need to think differently and more deeply, together with the awesome *courage* necessary to challenge the fashionable tidal undertow and resist 'group think' that dumbs everything down to the lowest common denominator. We must restrict our focus to the argument at hand and resist the temptation to assault the integrity of its advocate.

For the rules, three tests that we instinctively use in the trivia of every day will be helpful in your evaluation (they are outlined in more detail in the final chapter): *Is it rational? Is it real? How certain can I be?* To state the obvious, for something to be rational, there can be no contradictions and every effect must have a cause; something can only be real if it can be experienced through our senses. And there are several levels of certainty – we can be absolutely certain, or feel certain, or conclude that we are certain beyond reasonable doubt. Only after we undergo this process will we put our *faith* in something.

This critical process should help sift out mere *opinions*, defined by the *Oxford Dictionary* as 'judgements or beliefs based on grounds short of proof'. It also allows us to apply both our head and heart, which together influence our decision-making.

I urge you to reflect on the importance of asking the right questions of the right people as you proceed. To illustrate, you will notice that I am particularly indebted to three outstanding contemporary thinkers and writers who are often not heard above the noise – a lesson in itself: Dr RC Sproul, American philosopher and apologist, Dr Ravi Zacharias, Indian-born religious philosopher, and Dr John R W Stott, British biblical scholar and eminent clergyman. Having read their books and listened to them speak on many occasions, their blend of intellect, gentle touch and wit is compelling. For what it's worth, *Time* magazine recently included 84-year old Stott in its annual list of the world's most influential people for 2005. Noted for his modesty, he appears amongst an eclectic high profile group of people comprising the likes of Bill Clinton, Rupert Murdoch, the Dalai Lama, Bill Gates, Oprah Winfrey, Peter Singer, Clint Eastwood, and Nelson Mandela.

Finally, I have taken the liberty of sharing some personal conclusions in the Postscript, merely in the hope that you will be inspired to escape the rip of ever-changing conventional wisdom, and discover, or rediscover, how to think more deeply about improving your lot and make a lasting difference in our messed up world.

PART ONE

UNDERSTANDING
THE RIP

THE NEXT TIME you get on a plane, think about the navigator setting the direction. The challenge is similar to that of a swimmer in the rip of life – the positions of the departure and destination locations are set, and then allowance is made for the wind.

For those who are not mathematically inclined, 'position' is defined as the intersection between any two lines of an imaginary reference grid on the surface of the Earth. Longitude lines connect the north and south poles and latitude lines run parallel with the equator. Two numbers, called the position co-ordinates, are used to specify any location and are measured in degrees. The longitude line passing through Greenwich is deemed to be zero degrees, so any other line can be up to 180 degrees east or west of that line. Similarly, the line along the equator is set at zero degrees, and any parallel line can be up to 90 degrees north or south of that line.

'Direction' is defined as the angular difference, measured in degrees, from a *specified reference direction*. For true or magnetic bearings that means true or magnetic north. (The needle on a handheld compass points to magnetic north, whose location slightly differs from true north and continuously moves.) For relative bearings it means the heading or the nose of the aircraft. Fortunately, to allow for the wind the navigator has a sophisticated computer that calculates the 'drift angle' for the plane to point into the windward side.

Navigating an aircraft is a useful metaphor when considering how we set the direction of our journey at work and at home. Do you make decisions against a 'specified reference direction', and if so, how is it determined? In other words, what is the equivalent of true north around which your reference grid or framework is constructed? If you suspect that your world might revolve around the ebbs and flow of conventional wisdom, the following is an evaluation of how this informs decision-making, which draws heavily on the lessons of modern business – as already suggested, one of the most powerful influences on today's society.

Many of the deepest dilemmas confronting our torn world are brought to the surface, indicating that we are experiencing 'system failure' in the secular West. Prompted to seek new insights into how we can regain our true bearings, we then investigate what psychologists, neurologists and other masters of the mind think. Why? Because in our psychology-obsessed society, many believe that the answers lie within us.

If still perplexed, we can continue to follow our irresistible urge to rely even more on science, where very bright people and objectivity are expected to reign. Hence the evaluation of where cutting edge scientific thinking may be leading us in our quest for answers to the big questions.

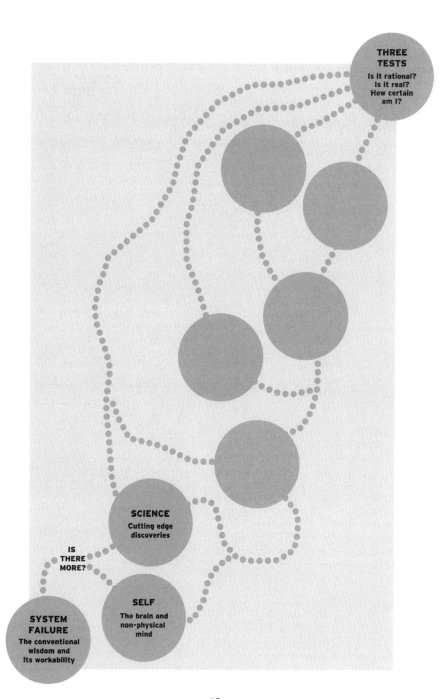

THREE TESTS
Is it rational?
Is it real?
How certain am I?

SCIENCE
Cutting edge discoveries

IS THERE MORE?

SELF
The brain and non-physical mind

SYSTEM FAILURE
The conventional wisdom and its workability

19

A case for intelligent design of the universe emerges, and when combined with the existence of morality, raises the tantalising question of whether there is an ultimate source, and hence an ultimate fixed reference point or reality.

CHAPTER ONE

SYSTEM FAILURE

APPRAISING THE CONVENTIONAL WISDOM
AND ITS WORKABILITY

Overview

Do you think there is a prevailing conventional wisdom or Western worldview that has largely determined your framework for making decisions? And if so, how would you characterise it? Decision-makers in organisations need systems to provide them with reliable information, so assuming you were the 'IT Director of the West', would you go so far as to advise that the 'operating system' is suffering a breakdown? Would you keep recommending more upgrades, or would you propose that a fresh start is the only solution?

I was taken to Sunday school as a child, which for most of you is a quaint relic of the past. So I grew up thinking this was the conventional wisdom, only to discover otherwise when I flew the nest. I began my radical challenge at university, by attending regular philosophical debates, dominated by over-confident young atheists, reading about other religions, and giving my local vicar a hard time.

The first part of my career involved marketing technical products, and our approach was mostly based on rational argument. When I moved to advertising 'consumer' products, we predominantly appealed to the desires of the heart. In my current role as a strategy consultant, my approach is more balanced, by keeping the left (for thinking) and right (for feeling) sides of the brain in sync. The 'heart' is liberated to dream and imagine, but the 'head' ensures people remain grounded in reality. This book tackles the big questions with the same approach.

For the most part, I have struggled with the many variants of the prevailing phenomenon known as secularism – the Latin root, *saeculum*, referring to this world in this time, the here and now. Social commentators tell us that during my lifetime the Western way has been in transition, from the 'modern' era of certainty and enlightenment, to the 'post-modern' era of uncertainty, disillusion and doubt. Increasingly we hear the cry 'I don't know anymore'.

The post-modernism school of thought has already become the gospel of business gurus and their massive followings. You will see that many observations in my analysis are made through the lens of modern business, where the idea that 'change is the only constant' permeates much of the contemporary thinking. Clearly this notion is exciting for a few and scary for the rest. The so-called no-nonsense approach to decision-making in the business world provides important insights into the workings of the Western secular system, as the line between what transpires outside office hours and what happens within the workplace has faded.

Modern corporations are ever raising the bar and espousing their version of how to think and behave, which is having an unparalleled influence on the way we operate in government, the community, and at home. In particular, geographical and cultural barriers have collapsed as technology and travel facilitate globalisation, allowing competition at all levels to flourish like never before. We are all caught up in the ensuing pressure.

We are constantly exhorted to strive for better and faster decision-making, greater performance with integrity, improved conflict resolution, more passionate commitment, and so on. Yet there is greater fragmentation. We look for solutions in education, yet there seems to be an apparent trend toward anti-intellectualism and loss of respect amongst the young. Tolerance is the watchword, yet it is leading to confusion, dysfunctional law and slippery slopes.

People are becoming more anxious, exasperated, introspective and individualistic, out to get the most they can for themselves, while uttering platitudes about the desperate need for everyone to make the world a better place. Bosses and workers, husbands and wives, and parents and children are operating from many differing premises, trying to harmonise contradictory views, attempting to change effects without attending to the underlying causes, and denying or misinterpreting reality.

Some still confidently assert that they are more and more certain, when I suspect in reality they may be attempting to mask a growing deep-seated lack of confidence and uncertainty. When the death sentence was pronounced on Salman Rushdie, he said:

> Doubt, it seems to me, is the central condition of a human being in the twentieth century. We cannot any longer have a fixed, certain knowledge of anything. Everything we know is pervaded by doubt and not by certainty.

The harder people try to fix the problems the bigger they seem to grow. Our materialistic, 'me at the centre' world, led by those who are more recognised for chintzy celebrity and charisma than character, appears to be not just off-track but on the wrong track.

Surely we have every good reason to challenge the very foundation of secularism – its denial of the transcendent and eternal – and the resultant preoccupation with the here and now. Is there something more that we can look forward to? If secularism is coming to the end of its shelf life, do we really want to succumb to a post-modern wave, a trend impossible to define, where reason disappears out the window and everything or anything goes?

To begin our search for clues, we follow a well-worn path by exploring our inner selves in Chapter 2.

Secularism

Sproul explains that a worldview usually emerges from competing elements of mythology, religion, politics and philosophy. Many in the West discard mythology, reject religion and opt out of politics, which leaves us with philosophy. But we still face the diversity of philosophical views and the question of whether there is a dominant one. Should we stop our search at pragmatism, utilitarianism or positivism? Or maybe existentialism or humanism is the answer? Or could it be pluralism, or relativism, or one of numerous other 'isms'?

The majority of today's 'isms' deny the transcendent and eternal, hence the overarching category called secularism. To help us apply the three tests, we will examine this phenomenon partly through the lens of Western business, the supposed Mecca of decision-making.

Different approaches to decision-making

The *Business Decisiveness Report* released recently by global consulting firm Capgemini, based on a survey of 270 senior executives within Britain's largest organisations, says that the top rated decision-making qualities are objectivity, listening carefully to others' opinions and setting clear criteria or standards and sticking to them. Bill Cook, Head of Consulting Services, Capgemini UK and Ireland commented:

> The ability to make decisions quickly, efficiently and effectively has always been at the heart of good business. Today we're all faced with greater choice, more competition and less time to consider our options or seek out the right advice. We hear so much about the negative consequences of 'choice anxiety' in our personal lives that it's little surprise we find parallels in the corporate world.

The secular response to this challenge is to adopt either a practical approach, or a more sophisticated scientific approach, to the decision-making process. Both have their attractions and inherent dangers.

The practical approach

In an environment where there are many dissenting views and pressing things to be done, we are inclined to put on hold the big questions and get down to the practicalities of solving immediate problems. 'If it works, just do it … forget about the theory … cut through the crap … be pragmatic' are sentiments that certainly accord with my Australian predisposition. My father could be very pragmatic. Tongue in cheek, he once said 'never marry for money, marry for love, but if she has money try to love her'. I only succeeded with the first part. He also said 'never tell a woman you love her until you want to marry her'. That I did succeed in doing, although forty years on I am still reminded of my excessive use of the word 'fond' in my courtship days.

Pragmatism says that it is perfectly OK for us to hold diametrically opposing views; let's just get on with it. But such expediency can lead to quick fixes, which merely create new problems, and so the wheel turns. Every end becomes the means to the next end, with never a final solution. There are many examples that spring to mind in all walks of life; let's just move from business to politics for a moment, and think about Saddam Hussein.

In 1983, Donald Rumsfeld, who went on to become the US Secretary of Defence, was sent to meet Saddam as a special envoy for President Reagan. The US was concerned about the Iran-Iraq war and, having decided that an Iranian victory would not serve its interests, began supporting Iraq. This was despite the knowledge that Iraq was using chemical weapons against Iran and its own Kurdish minority. But in the 1990s the world clamped down on Saddam, ensured his weapons were destroyed and imposed sanctions. Then Saddam stored and later unveiled piles of dead babies to show the humanitarian effect of sanctions. Meanwhile he used illicit oil deals, bribes and the oil-for-food billions to indulge his personal excesses, and accumulate enough money to re-equip his arsenal once sanctions were inevitably lifted.

In 2002, despite substantiated reports to the contrary, the US announced that Saddam had stockpiles of weapons of mass destruction, which posed an imminent and unacceptable threat to the international community, and launched a massive military offensive. The most recent consequence of US pragmatism is at the time of writing around 2,000 coalition deaths plus a guesstimate of around 25,000 civilian deaths, because 'we don't do body counts' according to General Tommy Franks. Violence begets violence. Skirmishes continue, more die almost every day, and as reports substantiate the absence of WMDs, the official justification for the pre-emptive strike on another country has shifted to 'the world is surely a better place without Saddam'. Both Saddam and the US have slithered a long way down their respective slippery slopes of pragmatism. (We will come back to slippery slopes shortly.)

The scientific approach

Some political leaders and business managers are more ponderous in their approach, and say things like 'we need proof that it works ... show us the facts and figures ... the devil is in the detail'. Such sentiments appeal to my desire to be logical, analytical and professional. However, pedantic people must beware when asserting that 'claims are only meaningful if they can be verified analytically or empirically'. This statement shoots itself in the foot, because it cannot be verified analytically or empirically – it is already an exception to its own rule. It is also too self-limiting, because there are many statements we consider very meaningful that cannot be verified in this manner. For example, when was the last time you said with passionate conviction 'I love you'?

A few years ago an ambitious Australian was promoted to Managing Director of the large UK business unit of a venerable British institution, known for its meticulous attention to detail. After many hours of impeccable presentations and intelligent debate at his first management team meeting, he suddenly realised no actionable decisions had been made and time was running out. Gripped with the fear of paralysis by analysis, he rushed through a host of decisions in rapid succession, and left feeling pretty good about his performance. He lasted about nine months before being handed a one-way ticket back home.

One of the morals of this story is to be wary of the dangers of an overly scientific approach, especially in helping us make sense of the future. Our complex risk analyses are only based on assumptions and estimated probabilities, determined by our past experience and personal propensity for risk.

Despite all the talk about this approach, students of business decision-making have concluded that decisions are not usually well founded on reason, but rather on a flash of inspiration, trial and error, or simply by sticking to what works. The new field of 'behavioural finance' reveals that people continually make the same errors of judgement, and behave differently according to how a situation is framed. They will take more risks to avoid losses than to make profits, and deliberately ignore evidence which conflicts with their opinion and select information that supports their view.

I cannot move on without making a passing reference to the 'blink approach', advocated by Malcolm Gladwell, in his book *Blink: the Power of Thinking without Thinking*. The novel concept of 'fast and frugal heuristics', or rules that are quick to apply when we have to make complex decisions quickly, with very little information, are the product of the Adaptative Behaviour and Cognition Group, at the Max Planck Institute for Human Development in Berlin. Their research findings suggest that trusting first impressions can lead to more successful outcomes than a more scientific approach. This revelation may be at least partially attributed to the obvious fact that irrelevant detail is not allowed to mislead or bog down the decision-making process in an era of unprecedented pressure. So where is this pressure coming from?

Pressures influencing decision-making

Competition

Although seen as 'good for the customer', the resultant life and death 'kill the competition' mantra causes a profound impact on our psyche. I suspect that many business techniques used to facilitate the relentless pursuit of winning at any cost (through greater speed, throughput and quality, all at a lower cost) are mostly treating the symptoms by relying metaphorically (and often literally) on quick fix stimulants, sedatives or painkillers. Anxiety prevails, and relationships have become urgent priorities. Notably, outstanding young career women have told me that they have lost any desire to invest in the time and cost involved in having relationships and children. Others say they simply cannot afford to do so.

Our health is at risk. In a recent National Stress Awareness Day in Britain, work-related stress was estimated to cost the economy £7 billion and 13 million working days a year. A striking statistic is the number of children on anti-depressants, as parents enter the race to see how early little Johnnie can read, piece his jigsaw together, spell, write and achieve remarkable physical feats.

Where have we gone wrong? One definition for the verb *to compete* says 'to strive against another or others to attain a goal', which is starkly opposed to the meaning of the Latin root *competere*, 'to strive together'. One leads to the zero sum game of *win:lose*, the other to the notion of co-operative competition, known as *win:win*. But when modern business leaders try to foster the latter, they must tackle a deeply entrenched competitive mindset that has permeated society, often at the expense of integrity.

Performance with integrity

In this cutthroat anxiety-ridden atmosphere, the call of leaders for the clarity and commitment required for greater 'performance with integrity' resonates. Policies and initiatives abound to restore lost 'social capital' and 'integrity' (a quick check on the Amazon website alone shows 890 titles with the word integrity incorporated). Integrity means wholeness, and according to Stott, for us to be whole, our mind, emotions, conscience and will must be in harmony. Perhaps dissonance at this deep level is the cause of so much confusion and anxiety, for example, why business leaders despair at their failure to make most 'change initiatives' work and why child rearing exasperates so many parents. Neither can be due to a dearth of 'How To' books or experts.

Surprisingly, even in our unprecedented era of technology and experience in running organisations, the age-old cry, 'we need better communications', together with the perceived need for 'presentation skills' training, remain firmly entrenched at the top of employee surveys. And if you are finding communications increasingly difficult, how do you fare when it comes to resolving outright conflicts?

Conflict resolution

Conflicting views become intractable when they emanate from competing frameworks. Frequently utilitarianism is the framework advanced as the practical way out, i.e. to seek the greatest 'good' for the greatest number. But what about those who lose out? And who decides what is good for whom and how?

One danger is that, in the absence of independent standards or principles, pragmatists point to what is accepted as 'the norm' to distinguish right from wrong. However the norm keeps changing as society moves on. There also seems to be confusion between the notions of *ethics* and *morals* as debates about complex moral issues rage, corporate scandals surface, and ethics courses and bodies proliferate. The Greek word for ethical is *ethos*, meaning character, and the Latin word for moral is *mos*, meaning custom. Sproul distinguishes them in terms of 'oughtness', what we should do, versus 'isness', what we are doing. Another distinction says ethics is the discipline of carefully reasoning what is right and wrong, whilst morality is a set of core beliefs about what is right and wrong. Blackburn, in his book *Ethics: A Very Short Introduction*, says 'an *ethical* climate is a different thing from a *moralistic* one. Indeed, one of the marks of an ethical climate may be hostility to moralizing, which is somehow out of place or bad form'. Are you any clearer?

Another danger in the confusion is the inclination to accept the views of 'experts' uncritically, because we assume that they are being objective. It is a small step from unquestioning compliance 'when the doctor says so', to deference to physicians and psychiatrists on matters beyond their area of expertise – even matters of life, death and morality. This is naïve; some of our best friends are very good doctors, but they are also human, with their own subjective tendencies just like the rest of us.

Hence, preferences of various elites can be adopted by, or even imposed on, the majority. Taken to the extreme, this eventuates in the tyranny of totalitarian systems and lack of justice for the vulnerable. But tyranny occurs beyond totalitarian regimes into emerging and mature democracies. In newly formed democracies the old guard is typically replaced by the tyranny of the rising wealthy, soon to be followed by the middle class. In the case of mature democracies, political leaders and leaders of highly respected corporations can collude to favour expediency over principle. An example is the profit-driven global media baron who wields unprecedented political power, through financial clout and biased journalism. This is ironic given that global media can also be the main hope for those with a passion for democracy.

Passion

Passion, and terms like courage and commitment, is central in the language of modern business and political leaders. They are inspiring, exciting words and, from my experience, the nobler the agreed purpose, the more potent they become. On day 1 of my first job I was told never to forget that I worked for the shareholder. Some years later the customer became king, and later still I was told that the employee is really number one. Eventually the stakeholder school revealed that we would only succeed if we looked after the interests of the shareholder *and* customer *and* employee. Not surprisingly, in our competitive world the pendulum is now back in favour of the shareholder. Meanwhile I have been swept up by the enthusiasm of advocates for other fashionable management fads, from total quality management, to process re-engineering and the balanced scorecard.

So, are the objects of our passion merely sales targets, shareholder value, customer satisfaction, employee motivation, or the latest performance improvement technique? Or are these in turn means to some greater common good, or even an ultimate end? In a recent article, Amanda Sinclair, Professor of Management at the Melbourne Business School, asserts that:

> This 'leadership' we are now so routinely fed, is seamlessly woven into a broader, and worrying, ideology ... consisting of that set of assumptions and beliefs about the virtues of capitalism and competition, instrumentalism and individualism that is beyond contestation ... The ideology is presented as truth ... The task of leaders becomes one of enforcing this truth, but is silent about the larger ends of all this effort and enterprise ... The language of leadership has become a dangerous and self-reinforcing discourse, dressing up the driving of overwork, relentless pressure and ruthless competition, in the guise of some higher values.

US shareholder activist Robert Monks, in his Canadian documentary *The Corporation*, dramatically depicts this growing disquiet about business. He compares a corporation to a shark:

> Each one is designed in a very efficient way to accomplish particular objectives. In the achievement of those objectives, there isn't any question of malevolence or of will. The enterprise has within it and the shark has within it those characteristics that enable it to do that for which it was designed.

Although these are widely held views and so must be taken very seriously, from my experience there are more than a few exceptions; for example I know many drug company employees who, with genuine compassion, devote their lives to finding new cures for dreadful diseases.

With the increased call for passion comes another apparent shift in the way we approach things: we used to be asked what we *think* and now it is more likely to be how we *feel*. Bookshelves are crowded with self-help books on feelings, including new concepts like 'emotional capital' and 'emotional intelligence'. But it is a small step to the moral code *if it feels good it is good*, which raises the spectre of a complex system of thought labelled existentialism, with many different shades and implications.

Existentialists are more concerned with *existence*, not some abstract idea of a higher *essence*. The word 'exist' means 'to be', and philosophers have long argued that of the three states of this verb, *being*, *becoming* and *non-being*, we can only be described as *becoming*, because of the constantly changing state of nature. And in answer to the question – becoming from what to what? – their answer is, nothing to nothing. Jean Paul Sartre, in his novel *Nausea*, takes this view to its logical conclusion by describing humanity as a useless passion, while Heidegger's idea of 'throwness' (Geworfenheit) also assumes that we have been hurled into a hostile universe to make our own way between points of nothingness.

In case you hope that we are now more enlightened, only last week an article about 'happiness' appeared (appropriately) in the 'Wellbeing' section of the *Sunday Age* magazine. Prof Robert Spillane, who teaches philosophy to aspiring business managers at the Macquarie University's Graduate School of Management, said this in a panel discussion: 'I think living is hurling yourself against the wall that is life. You keep hurling yourself until finally the wall is stronger than you and down you go. But what a way to go.' Is this a popular form of masochism that at least partly explains the extraordinarily high ratings enjoyed by Donald Trump's cringe-making television series, *The Apprentice*?

Leading behavioural economists Prof Ted O'Donoghue, Cornell University, and Prof Matthew Rabin, University of California, Berkeley, demonstrate how such a mindset can be translated to an 'economics of immediate gratification':

> There is a mass of evidence that people are characterised by a preference for immediate gratification and self-control problems.
>
> We ... have shown how such preferences give rise to procrastination, over-indulgence in addictive activities, seemingly excessive punishments for delay in completing a task, and over-consumption of basic consumer goods.

Where has our passion for immediate gratification left us? We need look no further than the resultant explosion in debt, with its debilitating consequences. Only fifty years ago my father was a dream client of the local bank manager, because he very rarely went into the red, and had sleepless nights when he could not avoid it. He would be of little interest to the modern 'relationship manager' and credit card marketer, because he only bought what he could pay for on the spot, and certainly would have recoiled against the alluring call to buy now and pay later.

We cannot finish our brief discussion on existentialism without mentioning its contradictory nature. You might feel I am being a bit harsh by using as an example the youth slogans in the sixties: 'do your own thing' and 'tell it like it is'. They simultaneously called for 'free love' with no private responsibility; for a world without killing except for the unborn; and for an environment free of toxic substances except for those they used on themselves. Today's generation is now dealing with the legacy of these youthful, unbridled passions of its immediate forebears. Almost daily we read of schools increasingly crippled by rampant under-age sex, drug use, teenage drunkenness, and violence.

Fragmentation

In a charged atmosphere of contradictory claims and demands, cynicism and fragmentation are endemic in the workplace; notwithstanding enormous amounts of money and effort being invested in trying to persuade millions of employees to 'buy in' to shared corporate missions, visions, values, and other ideals. Here are just two examples where senior managers appear to take corporate values very seriously.

Samuel J Palmisano was appointed CEO of IBM in 2002, and launched a major corporate values initiative in 2003. He was then interviewed by Paul Hemp and Thomas A Stewart, as recorded in 'The HBR Interview: Leading Change When Business Is Good', *Harvard Business Review*, December 2004. IBM conducted a three-day forum on its intranet, called ValuesJam, where 50,000 employees evaluated a proposed alternative to the company's three Basic Beliefs laid out by the founder in 1914. Palmisano says these beliefs 'had become part of the problem', i.e. 'respect for the individual' became entitlement, and 'the best customer service' and 'pursuit of excellence' became arrogance.

A small team finally crafted three new corporate values, based on an analysis of the massive employee input:

Dedication to every client's success
Innovation that matters – for our company and for the world
Trust and personal responsibility in all relationships

Palmisano said that these values would help provide balance between the need for immediate profit and the long-term relationship. He also said the debate was not so much about the values themselves, but whether IBM is willing and able to live them.

Employee reactions ranged from gushing enthusiasm to scornful cynicism.

The second example is for a very different kind of business. According to The Body Shop website:

> The core principles that define our ethical approach to business are organised into five pillars: Defend Human Rights, Protect Our Planet, Support Community Trade, Activate Self-Esteem, and Against Animal Testing. These principles form the basis of our campaigns and community programmes, as well as our ethical policies and guidelines.

Make of these well-meaning initiatives what you will, but the reality for many is the relentless, unrealistic and often conflicting demands of shareholders, bosses, and customers. Greed is perceived to rule. Some time ago I read how the CEO of a big bank was backing a major internal programme to transform the culture, and hence performance, of his business. But only months later, thousands of employees went out on strike; their patience had run out. Although a favourite target, banks are not much different from any other organisation. I have reluctantly concluded that real sustainable change in any organisation will only flow from deep changes within each individual, and today a huge number of employees simply feel disenfranchised.

It is my experience that loyalty has fast become an out-dated notion, whether it is to your organisation, boss, employees or customer (and bank, spouse, parent or Prime Minister for that matter). People are treating their current employment merely as a stepping-stone in their career progression, and are retreating into their microcosm. The things that get them out of bed are the relationships they have with their immediate colleagues, team members and customers, the intrinsic value they ascribe to their particular product, service or project, the personal development opportunities their jobs provide, and the financial reward and recognition they receive. Although loyalty to immediate colleagues is laudable, the resultant fragmentation of organisations makes them unmanageable by conventional methods.

In the absence of absolutes, is the root cause of fragmentation, both in business and society, the secularist's necessity to live with pluralism and relativism? Because the concept of relativity was originally intended to describe motion, it seems a rather limited foundation on which to build a school of thought that says *everything is relative*. Only this week an intelligent young man told me this was his mantra, and either could not or would not concede that this is yet another statement that makes nonsense of itself, and every other statement, axiom and law, because by definition they must all be relative. The inevitable conclusion is that there can be no ultimate reference point. No Truth, only truths, no Purpose, only purposes and no Value, only values.

When we eliminate Truth or principles, there is a vacuum created, and it will be filled by the preferences of the most powerful, passionate, strident, or subtle. Professing humanists are strongly committed to values, which are mostly derived from religious sources but deliberately divorced from their theological source. Such preferences may be emotionally appealing for those who want to extract some meaning out of life, but without sure foundations they are no more than sentiment. Nuclear physicist and theologian, Ian Barbour, in an interview with *Financial Times* journalist Christian Tyler, said 'any flower cut from its roots will last for awhile.'

Humanists dream of Utopia, a world made better primarily through education, technology and industry, believing that the conservatism of religion holds back our entire race. Although on the wane, is this pervasive view why organisations around the world pay thousands of well-meaning consultants and HR people, frequently self-confessed humanists, to create their own special concoction of corporate creeds? And why many political leaders play safe by carefully projecting themselves as humanists rather than adherents to religious principles?

By the way, did you know that the Greek for *utopia* means 'nowhere'? The word was invented by English scholar and humanist, Sir Thomas More, born in 1477, beheaded in 1535, and canonised in 1935. In his famous book of the same name, More compares the social and economic conditions of Europe with those of a fictional, unattainable ideal society, located on an island off the New World. Sadly the literal meaning and origin of words are no longer given the emphasis they deserve by today's educationalists. Take for example the oft overlooked and fundamental distinction between *humanitarianism*, showing philanthropic concern for our fellowman, and humanism, declared a religion by the US Supreme Court in 1961 and considered by some to be the 'official religion of the US'.

Education

Well-meaning humanists pervade our schools, where much of the foundations for sound decision-making are laid. As exemplars, teachers make many important choices about 'what is best', but as they are human like the rest of us, they will be influenced by their own view of life. One of the wonders of being my age is to observe our first baby grandchild grow and become his own little person, immensely loved by his parents, whose burning desire is to provide him with the very best opportunities. At school he will be fortunate to experience the most advanced techniques to develop the many essential skills for life. But will he be inspired and equipped to challenge the prevailing conventional wisdom of his day, in an objective and thorough way?

Will all those who teach him aim to be consistent with the kind of package his parents hope to shape out of this little life, even if they adhere to different views? Or will humanism, or some other 'ism', triumph by default? Interestingly, in the Australian State of Victoria, current legislation (first enacted in 1872) that bans any teacher from giving any instruction other than secular is being re-written to allow teachers to discuss religion. At the same time, some are heralding a revolution in teaching 'higher-order thinking skills', known as 'philosophy for children'. Janette Poulton, education officer at the Victorian Association for Philosophy in Schools, says: 'A lot of common assumptions are faulty and obsolete and need to be re-examined … It can help equip people to deal with propaganda and avoid being manipulated by others.'

I wonder how many parents even think to debate these issues with the teachers of their children, and whether we have handed over too much responsibility. Pru Goward, the Australian Federal Sex Discrimination Commissioner, says that parents must take on the responsibility for educating their children about sex, because teachers will only get into trouble for 'not teaching values or teaching the wrong ones'. Although acknowledging that a few parents might 'urge abstinence on religious and moral grounds … only very hopeful parents would believe any of this is the end of the conversation'. In her opinion, education about sex and its potential outcomes is the best bet to lower abortion levels. Similarly, education is advocated as the primary means to combat escalating bullying by children and parental intimidation of teachers, but Jan Shrimpton, an Australian school principal at the coalface, recently said: 'There's an expectation that we will have the answers because we're educationalists. Well we've got some of the answers, but we can't fix the whole of society.'

The question of values in schools was put on the agenda in Australia earlier this year, when the Prime Minister, John Howard, said that the drift of students to private schools was partly because government schools were 'values neutral'. But is such a state possible?

The propensity to fabricate 'mission and values' statements is not restricted to the corporate world. Five years ago, the Victorian Curriculum and Assessment Authority proposed a list of ten values, which generated much debate, and it recently announced five principles to be taught in all Victorian schools next year: learning for all, pursuit of excellence, engagement and effort, respect for evidence, and openness of mind. It is interesting that only one of the original ten, pursuit of excellence, made the final list. Examples of those left out include tolerance and understanding, respect, social justice and freedom.

The Minister for Education, Lynne Kosky, acknowledged that some would disagree with the principles, but they were 'almost indisputable' for those in a democracy. The head of the Independent Education Union of Victoria, Tony Keenan, described them as 'just a statement of the bleeding obvious', and noted the academic focus. I wonder what values the Prime Minister had in mind. In commenting on these principles Warwick McFadyen, a journalist for Australian newspaper *The Age*, wrote: 'Our children need role models they can respect, such as politicians. In your dreams!'

Fortunately respected role models do abound. I recently listened to an inspiring presentation by a much-loved schoolteacher, who has made his mission to help those children rejected by the system because they won't perform and conform. Some cannot read or write at the age of thirteen, and because of being repeatedly sent out of the classroom they take to the streets and resort to vandalism and worse. By introducing an innovative practical component to the curriculum, he has kept these children in their school and off the streets; they have learned to read and write, assimilate back into the community, and take up gainful employment. He says such children are destructive because they are angry, and instead of telling them they are bad, the system must be adapted to meet their needs; but most importantly, he says, *they must be loved*.

Our grandchild may go on to tertiary education, where young people are largely left to their own devices to digest, process and make sense of a vast array of contradictory ideas. Academic disciplines have proliferated and become more and more specialised and introspective in their approach. The word 'university' originally meant a place out of which unity could coexist with diversity. It was intended to help young people gain a *coherent* understanding of life, through observing the overlaps and intricate interactions of the many different fields. Today, there are very few departments that encourage collaboration across disciplines. Consequently, the incubator available to the leaders who insist that those under their stewardship must take a holistic approach to business and government is merely a 'multiversity'.

Is our so-called open-minded, values neutral approach to education actually the opposite? Is this a reason why many believe that anti-intellectualism, a major enemy of 'joined-up thinking', appears to be on the rise? Immediately the stereotypical teenager comes to mind, constantly switching from his PlayStation, to online chat, downloading music, and texting his mates. For him, books are boring. I was faintly amused when an author recently gave me a copy of his new book, which he said was written for the majority who don't read books any more.

But just to muddy the water, do you realise how many kids are reading extraordinarily lengthy and convoluted tales about Harry Potter's exploits? And did you know that IQ scores are actually rising? It is surmised that the skills obtained in today's 'screen culture', through rapidly processing information from an early age, will help achieve higher scores in the kind of tests used to measure IQ. In fact we might be producing a new generation of much needed problem-solvers.

What can we learn from these complex trends in our education system and the behaviour of our youth? Many could start by thinking more deeply about the implications, and being more tolerant of those with contrary views.

Tolerance

To co-exist in our diverse world, and to pay more than lip service to the assertion of business leaders that 'our only asset is our people', we must be tolerant (or even, dare I say, respectful) of each other. Tolerance has become a watchword for our wider secular society, but as I inferred earlier when mentioning pragmatism and utilitarianism, how far should we take this lofty sentiment? When the pluralist says morality is relative and we cannot tolerate one group imposing its views on others, must we conclude that all views are equally tolerable and equally valid, even when they are contradictory?

Stott helpfully distinguishes between three kinds of tolerance. Legal tolerance, which rightly ensures that everyone has the freedom to profess, practise and propagate his or her political and religious beliefs. Social tolerance, which rightly encourages respect for all persons and an understanding of their position. And intellectual tolerance, which for Stott is different: 'To cultivate a mind so broad that it can tolerate every opinion is not a virtue; it is the vice of the feeble-minded.'

Social tolerance is often confused with intellectual tolerance. Ironically, in our educated world of so-called tolerance, it seems extraordinarily easy to whip the crowd into a state of irrational, hateful frenzy. I will not forget the endless dinner party speculation and bile poured out on Lindy Chamberlain, the Australian Seventh Day Adventist who claimed a dingo had taken her baby from a remote campsite. Even though an appeal court finally exonerated her of murder, it took the Schepisi film, *A Cry in the Dark* (*Evil Angels* in the US), and a fine performance by Meryl Streep, to put this dreadful episode to rest.

In a similar vein, we are very familiar with the phenomenon

known as road rage. I was surprised to discover recently how this has now evolved into 'ramp rage'. We unload our small boat at a public launching ramp, where fistfights have erupted, would you believe, between guys who are desperate to go fishing and presumably have a relaxing peaceful time!

When many groups demanding their rights confuse us, it is sometimes easier to opt out and rely on the government to create legislative solutions to moral dilemmas. Gregory Hywood, former editor-in-chief of *The Age*, says that, in today's elections, 'the politics of values and politics of wealth will be decisive in determining who prevails'. But can we rely on governments to make value judgements when many are convinced that politics and values are mutually incompatible? In regard to our apparent impotence in the face of atrocities like those in Sudan, Simon Tisdall, a commentator for *The Guardian*, says that 'Western leaders are all hat and no cattle'. He must have come from the bush, where the bloke with the biggest hat sometimes had the smallest herd.

So how do we vote? On the highly emotive issue of abortion, there are seemingly three positions – pro-life, pro-abortion and pro-choice: 'I personally would not have an abortion because I believe it is wrong, but every woman should have the right to make that choice for herself.' But practically there are only two alternatives, because the pro-choice vote amounts to a pro-abortion vote. The pro-choice position poses as an argument for *legal* rights, but in actuality the issue is about *moral* rights. Assuming there is 'right' and 'wrong', we look to our justice system to determine the legal distinction, but who should determine the moral distinction? Recently, Justice Frank Vincent, who has been an Australian Supreme Court judge for 20 years, said in an interview with Fergus Shiel: 'On occasion, someone insists on their legal rights and all of the moral arguments favour the other party, but it would be a betrayal of the oaths of office to determine the case on the basis of how you would like to see it resolved'.

Once the two are confused, further confusion follows. Even though scientists cannot agree on when life begins in the womb, the abortion debate has already moved on to the issue of 'late stage termination', ironically the same foetal age at which we are now able to save premature babies, thanks to vast expenditure and resultant advances in medical technology. Moreover, legislative reform is being advocated to allow obstetric hospitals to protect unborn children where there are grounds to believe that the child is at risk, for example where the mother is drug dependent.

Another example of this kind of confusion arises from the controversial issue of euthanasia, as pioneered in the Netherlands. There was a recent high profile case in the US, which involved a protracted legal battle regarding a severely brain-damaged young woman, kept alive via a feeding tube. Her husband claimed she would have wanted to die and her parents disagreed. There are several notable aspects about this tragic case, in addition to the fact that the disabled woman had been unable to express herself. She was alive, but totally dependent on others to feed her; she was not on 'artificial life support'. Some doctors pronounced her to be in a 'persistent vegetative state' whilst others claimed she 'had a consciousness'. The majority in the House of Representatives and the President held that she should continue to be fed, although 59% of American 'evangelical Christians' disagreed with the House and their President.

Much of the debate was played out at the emotional rather than rational level. For example, the attorney representing her husband called the House interference 'thuggery', and said she was 'a pawn in a political football game'. Incredibly, only one judge made the eventual ruling: that her feeding tube should be removed, for her to 'die naturally'. She was then starved to death.

All this occurred in a country where the most basic 'civil right' is the right to life; even starving a dog to death would attract a severe penalty.

Other examples of similar confusion abound. Take for instance the Racial and Religious Tolerance Act, enacted in 2001 by the Victorian government to provide for both civil complaints and criminal offences. This law was justified by the need to maintain civil order as tensions build in a growing multicultural society. It was painstakingly developed through a comprehensive consultative process, in an attempt to allow for numerous anticipated complexities. For instance, there is a crucial distinction made between 'robust discussion' and 'incitement of hatred and contempt'. Concerned about the mixing of racial and religious vilification, Catholic Archbishop Denis Hart is quoted in an article by Barney Zwartz of *The Age* that: 'We want robust dialogue by adherents of particular religions, but not in a way that gathers up race.'

The first case, only recently put before the court, has raised a number of questions. As society becomes more complex is it inevitable that we will have more laws? If so, what will be the impact on our general mood and demeanour – will the letter of the law overwhelm the spirit of the law? How *legally* pedantic must the ordinary person be in his or her behaviour, e.g. will some people find it difficult to draw the line between robust discussion and the risk of incitement, particularly where passion prevails and humour is used? Skilled lawyers might unequivocally and precisely respond to most of our legal questions, but they also counsel that any new law requires a time of testing and modification before its effectiveness can be fairly evaluated. Meanwhile, how do we weigh the need for this process against the potential cost incurred by the guinea pigs? And when new laws governing personal morality don't work, are we naturally inclined to make them tougher and more comprehensive?

Many assert that dysfunctional law is inevitable when legislation is extended beyond just protecting people and their property to controlling the way we behave. Today's anti-vilification laws only require an individual to claim offence to trigger a protracted and expensive process. Is this a downward path leading to outright fear of speaking up on any contentious moral issue? An editorial in *The Australian* newspaper commented:

> Along with privacy laws, trespass laws, nuisance laws and anti-discrimination laws, defamation laws in which truth by itself is no defence prop up a system of overt censorship and silent self-censorship ... The biggest winners of all, of course, have been the lawyers.

Is this what we want? Is it easier on the mind and conscience to declare all things subjective in the moral realm, rather than try to understand and evaluate differing moral frameworks and the consequences of our decisions, such as the way we vote? Or do we bury our heads in the sand? The recently screened British documentary, *My Foetus*, provoked an outcry about the graphic filming of an abortion. Many said such 'gruesome confronting' material was offensive and should not be shown on television. Others said it forced them to 'confront the big question'. Have we become so hardened that we need this kind of stimulus to prompt some kind of meaningful debate?

Society can only reverse these trends by proactively encouraging fearless, open and constructive argument about the big questions. It is perplexing how the behaviour of proponents of tolerance often does not accord with the literal meaning of being tolerant: 'to allow to exist without interference or molestation'. The loss of respect across society was very high on the agenda of the latest British election, and perhaps this is perversely related to the emphasis on tolerance. I read yesterday of a disturbingly high incidence of physical abuse by teenagers against their parents. Those who bear the brunt of scoffing, dismissal and even physical abuse, tend to be people brave enough to take a moral stand against the downward path.

Slippery slopes

There are numerous instances where acquiescence to even apparently minor issues, actions or laws can be the start of a dangerous downward path. But many ridicule the 'slippery slope argument', by asserting that we are smart enough to trust our ability to make sound judgements, step by step, as we move forward. And, because of the multiplicity of potential outcomes, fear of making mistakes will just lead to paralysis.

A classic example is the current hotly debated issue of torture. Law professor Mirko Bagaric, head of the Deakin Law School in Australia and co-author of a paper 'Not Enough Official Torture in the World?', just published in the *University of San Francisco Law Review*, counters the slippery slope argument with the assertion that 'legalisation in very rare circumstances' would in fact reduce instances of this already widespread practice.

Another law professor, Eugene Volokh at UCLA School of Law, in his article 'The Mechanisms of the Slippery Slope' published in a recent *Harvard Law Review*, warns that slippery slopes are a real risk. For example he describes the 'attitude-altering slippery slope' that starts with a small step and progressively desensitises people to go along with further steps. He says that, because of lack of time or expertise to consider a matter fully, we tend conveniently to assume that if something is the law it probably ought to be the law, and then support still more sweeping versions.

For the same reasons we tend to concentrate on the big changes and defer to the government or elite opinion for the seemingly small ones, thus opening the way for big changes that we do not support to be implemented in apparently innocuous small steps. This process of desensitisation is likened to the parable of the frog in hot water – when dropped into boiling water it will jump out, but put it in cold water and slowly raise the temperature and it will eventually cook.

The issue of euthanasia is a good example of the very real dangers of the slippery slope. Every day older people in great distress are offered the option. Three years ago a close Dutch friend of ours was diagnosed with a nasty form of cancer. A top American oncologist was brutally candid about his dismal prognosis, but added how fortunate he was to be born in Holland, where euthanasia is legal. Our friend was gob-smacked, and fortunately defied the doctors with a fighting recovery. He was only in his fifties; so how old do you need to be?

Wesley J Smith recently wrote in the American *Daily Standard* about the state of medical ethics in the Netherlands, where doctors are now officially allowed to 'euthanise' children under twelve, if they believe their suffering is intolerable or if they have an incurable illness. As Smith writes:

> For anyone paying attention to the continuing collapse of medical ethics in the Netherlands, this isn't at all shocking … Doctors were (already) killing approximately 8 percent of all infants who died each year in the Netherlands … Of these, one-third would have lived more than a month. At least 10 to 15 of these killings involved infants who did not require life-sustaining treatment to stay alive. The study found that a shocking 45 percent of neo-natologists and 31 percent of paediatricians who responded to questionnaires had killed infants.

Smith adds that at least a fifth of the killings were performed without parental consent, and goes on to ask:

Why does accepting euthanasia as a remedy for suffering in very limited circumstances inevitably lead to never-ending expansion of the killing license? Blame the radically altered mindset that results when killing is redefined from a moral wrong into a beneficent and legal act. If killing is right for, say, the adult cancer patient, why shouldn't it be just as right for the disabled quadriplegic, the suicidal mother whose children have been killed in an accident, or the infant born with profound mental retardation? There can be little doubt anymore that the 'slippery slope' of euthanasia has turned into an avalanche.

It is intriguing to note the number of commentators who are adamant that we need to persist with our current system, rather than objectively consider a radical alternative. For example, in an article published in *The Age*, Thornton McCamish argues against 'moral certainty', almost with a contemptuous tone. His proposed alternative is 'secular democracy', which he says 'can offer only the certainty that together, the citizens of a nation can fumble their way towards certain normative values as enshrined in our laws; and that when the values of the people change, the laws will change with them'.

Cardinal Ratzinger, the newly elected Pope, warns of an inherent danger in today's liberal consensus, which he observes has evolved into a 'worrying and aggressive' ideology: 'Secularism is no longer that element of neutrality, which opens up space for freedom for all. It is beginning to change into an ideology which, through politics, is being imposed.'

But as we have meandered through the miasma of today's world, how can anyone make an ideology out of these shifting riptides? One way out of this dilemma is to reach back to the past, as illustrated by the Australian Education Minister, Dr Brendan Nelson. He reminds his fellow citizens of their legendary forefathers' exploits at Gallipoli, and says their defining characteristics should include 'mateship' and giving others a 'fair go'. He also says that people who 'don't want to live by Australian values ... can basically clear off'. Predictably he has drawn fire from many quarters in this diverse society, not least because nearly one in four was born overseas.

Another way out is to junk the past. Enter the post-modernists, who say that the era of modernity, with its false promise of utopianism, has come to an end; and the future is about making it up as we go.

Post-modernism

There are numerous attempts to explain this phenomenon, often emanating from the arts world. To illustrate, I will take just one example. Glenn Ward, artist and lecturer in visual culture, explains what he thinks post-modernism is about, in his book by that name:

> [It] allows ideas to stay mobile, constantly re-inventing themselves and adjusting to changing circumstances.
> [It is] most usefully thought of as an elastic critical category with a range of applications and potential understandings. It is a kind of 'portable' term which enables us to enter a great many ideas about the specific characteristics of the world today.

Ward says these ideas can be divided up in various ways, one being in terms of the 'ends' or 'deaths' that it signals:

- The end of history – this relates to scepticism about the idea of progress, debates about the way histories are written and the thought that events lack unity or direction.

- The end of man – this relates to the interrogation of mankind as a social and historical invention and the idea that new technologies are taking us into a post-human stage of development.
- The death of the real – this relates to abandonment of the pursuit of absolute truth and preference for the temporary, superficial and apparent.

This school of thought is gaining momentum, so what are the implications? Fundamentally, words have no objective meaning, only how you or I interpret them, or what we want them to mean. Hence any conversation can have more than one meaning, which renders it meaningless, along with books written by Ward and this author. It also spells the death knell for words like rationality, reality and certainty, and the respective tests.

Martin Robinson concludes that post-modernism is not a reaction to modernism, but rather its logical outcome. He states the obvious in what we might conclude is yet another meaningless book, The Faith of the Unbeliever:

> The unmasking of the real concern of both modernism and post-modernism demonstrates very clearly that the ultimate end of a commitment to nothing but reason is in fact irrationality.

Do you think we are experiencing 'system failure' at the root of our decision-making at work and at home?

CHAPTER TWO

SELF

DISTINGUISHING BETWEEN THE BRAIN
AND THE NON-PHYSICAL MIND

Overview

What is your reaction to the increasing reliance on psychology to inform our decisions? The conventional wisdom says that many of our problems start from within, and can be overcome from within. What do you make of the view held by the modern psychologists who say that the focus on self-realisation supersedes the notion of evil, which is simply based on ignorance?

If, like most of us, you distinguish between good and bad behaviour, what do you make of the implication that evil and an independent standard must exist? Some brilliant thinkers use reason and experience to conclude that above and beyond the ordinary facts of our behaviour there is some kind of a moral law, which none of us invented. If so, where does this law come from?

An even bigger mystery might be why we sense we ought to obey this law. What is within us that seems to urge us to behave in a certain way, and makes us uncomfortable when we don't? Do all the answers lie in the physical brain?

Conventional wisdom says that the brain evolved from matter like everything else, so at a certain level of structure and complexity we must have become conscious and developed a mind. But how did *that* happen? What is more, how does this unique organism, comprising ten thousand million cells and a thousand million million connections, actually enable us to absorb knowledge, formulate ideas, make decisions, meditate, and fall in love?

You will see in the analysis that science and personal experience point to the possibility of humans having a non-physical self, which interacts with, but is separate from, their physical brain. So where does this essence of human life come from?

Prompted by the apparent existence of morality, an initial examination of differing scientific views leads us to take a closer look in Chapter 3 at where cutting edge science may be pointing in regard to the origin of the non-physical and physical. I am particularly indebted to investigative journalist Lee Strobel for his interviews with a diverse range of scientists .

Goodness and badness

There is an unprecedented inclination to turn to psychology and its practitioners for solutions to problems and answers to the big questions. Theodore Roszak, Professor of History at California State University and writer on eco-psychology, represents many in this field when he says that we need to 'awaken to the god who sleeps at the root of our human being'. It is about finding yourself; to know yourself is to know the god within; self realisation is god realisation.

The popular psychology of Abraham Maslow and Carl Rogers, the two leaders of the human potential movement, says human beings are not characterised by pathology, as Freud said, but by potential – what they may become. They are capable of self-actualisation and are even capable of self-transcendence –

there is no limit to what they may become. And there is more to the story. Rogers says that humans are inherently good and that evil is nothing but ignorance of our identity and potential. How does this view align with your observation of the 'human condition'?

Most believe that there is both good and bad in us. Hugh Mackay, eminent Australian psychologist and social researcher with formidable insights into modern culture, says in his recent book *Right and Wrong*:

> You can find within yourself the answers to questions like 'What should I do?' or 'How should I live?' or even 'What's the point of trying to do the right thing?'
>
> Morality isn't a set of rules or even a road map: it's a way of travelling, a mindset, a resource for the journey.
>
> Goodness is not a destination; it is more like the calibration of true north on a compass, maintaining our sense of direction while leaving us free to explore whatever lies ahead.

Mackay clearly assumes that there is such a thing called 'morality', and offers practical tips on the process of making moral choices in various situations that are 'right for you'. But where do our guiding values come from? Mackay says: 'Our moral values spring directly from the experience of learning how to live with other people.' C S Lewis, the brilliant writer and communicator, who after years at Oxford became Professor of Mediaeval and Renaissance Literature at Cambridge, implies that our moral values spring from a deeper well. Lewis addresses the question of how much we are influenced by factors like 'instincts', cultural differences and social convention. He weaves these factors with other arguments, to support his conclusion that above and beyond us there is an independent 'Moral Law'.

Instincts

Lewis refutes the idea that any moral sense can be simply attributed to instinct, by explaining that, if there were only instincts, the stronger would prevail. This is frequently not the case, however, when humans are prompted to follow the weaker impulse. For example, if we hear a person in danger cry for help, we react with two desires – to give help (the herd instinct) and to keep away (self-preservation instinct). But a third impulse urges us to follow the desire to help and suppress the desire to escape.

Also, if the Moral Law were instinctive, we would have to assume that some instincts are good and others bad. Lewis uses the piano metaphor to illustrate his conclusion that 'the Moral Law tells us the tune (called goodness or right conduct) we have to play; our instincts are merely the keys'. Hence it depends on the occasion whether an impulse is either encouraged or suppressed. For example, there are times when a mother's love for her children or a man's love for his country have to be suppressed or they will lead to unfairness to other people's children or homelands.

Cultural differences

Many say that different civilisations and different ages have had quite different moralities, so it is untrue to claim that there is a universal Moral Law. However, after examining the diverse moral teachings of the ancient Egyptians, Babylonians, Hindus, Chinese, Greeks and Romans, Lewis concluded that 'there have been differences between their moralities, but these have never amounted to anything like a total difference'. He appealed to our personal experience, and having worked and socialised with people from around the world, I observe vastly more agreement than disagreement about what is fair and decent.

Social convention

Others say that what is described as Moral Law is actually no more than social convention, learned through education. Lewis disagrees, first because of his observation that the differences in morality between cultures and eras are not great, while cultural conventions like road rules and dress may vary to any extent. And second, we think that certain moralities are better or worse than others, which implies that we are measuring them by some independent standard. Lewis says that a person does not call a line crooked unless he has some idea of a straight line.

He argues that there are two kinds of 'laws': those of *physical* nature, like gravity, and those of *human* nature, which Lewis calls fair play, decent behaviour, morality or simply Right and Wrong. In fact the former may not really be laws in the strict sense, but simply a way of describing the way the universe behaves – 'what Nature, in fact, does'. In the latter case, we are referring to 'what humans *ought* to do' but commonly don't. We know that we cannot defy the physical laws but are free to disobey the laws of human nature. And we are troubled when we do, as demonstrated by our readiness to make excuses when found out.

Lewis says there are two facts at the foundation of all clear thinking about ourselves and the universe in which we live:

First, that human beings all over the Earth, have this curious idea that they ought to behave in a certain way, and cannot really get rid of it. Secondly, that they do not in fact behave in that way.

Let's dig deeper to see what scientists have to say about the immediate *source* of our thinking, the phenomenon we call consciousness.

Consciousness

Much of today's thinking about 'the god within' has been influenced by Darwin. If Darwin is right, it seems plausible that with enough of the right structure and complexity, a futuristic computer will eventually gain consciousness, or a mind of its own. But from my daily experience of crashes, error messages, email overload and the invaluable help of my 'techie', I would like to think John Searle, Professor of the Philosophy of Mind and Language, University of California, Berkeley, is closer to the mark when he says: 'You can expand the power all you want, hooking up as many computers as you think you need, and they still won't be conscious, because all they'll ever do is shuffle symbols.' Searle then seems to contradict himself when he says 'in my worldview, consciousness is caused by brain processes'.

When one-time atheist Strobel asked Prof J P Moreland (BSc in Chemistry, ThM in Theology, and a PhD in Philosophy, University of Southern California) what some implications of us being solely physical might be, he suggested three. First, there would be no consciousness, 'because if everything is physical, it could be described entirely from a third-person point of view ... yet we know that we have first-person, subjective points of view'. Second, he said there would be no free will, 'because matter is completely governed by the laws of nature'. And third, he said there would be no disembodied state, instanced by many near-death experiences reported by people who had been clinically dead.

Moreland also pointed out that scientists can monitor physical brain activity whilst someone is dreaming, but they have to wake up the person to know what he or she is dreaming about, 'because conscious states have the feature of being inner and private, but the brain's states don't'. He also makes the philosophical point that, unlike mental states, brain states are not *about* anything.

For example, no brain states are true or false, so how can the physical brain help the scientist make this distinction?

Here is an intriguing question to pose to scientists who assert that the answers lie solely in the physical brain: how can they determine what is true? J B S Haldane, British biologist and evolutionist, seems challenged by this question:

> If my mental processes are determined wholly by the motions of the atoms in my brain, I have no reason to suppose that my beliefs are true … and hence I have no reason for supposing my brain to be composed of atoms.

There should be no surprise that many philosophers and scientists are now of the view that the laws of physics and chemistry cannot explain human consciousness. Instead, in addition to the visible, physical brain, an invisible non-physical ego, self, or soul contains our invisible consciousness and animates our body. The body and self are separate entities, making up the duality of personhood. Hence the age-old school of thought known as 'dualism', where mind and body, or spirit and matter, are distinct. (Incidentally, others still hold to another view that everything is one, known as 'monism'.)

After operating on over a thousand epilepsy patients, Wilder Penfield, the pioneering father of neurosurgery, once described as the greatest physician ever, concluded in *The Mystery of the Mind*:

> To expect the highest brain mechanism or any set of reflexes, however complicated, to carry out what the brain does, and thus perform all the functions of the mind, is quite absurd … What a thrill it is, then, to discover that the scientist, too, can legitimately believe in the existence of the spirit.

If, as Moreland says, 'I *am* a soul, and I *have* a body', and if, as revolutionary philosopher René Descartes said many years ago, 'I think, therefore I am', it is reasonable to ask 'who am I' and 'where do I come from?'

.

CHAPTER THREE

SCIENCE

BEING BLINDED OR ILLUMINED BY
CUTTING EDGE DISCOVERIES

Overview

Do you subscribe to today's conventional wisdom that the universe started from nothing with a random big bang and, as hypothesised by Darwin in his *Origin of Species*, life has gradually evolved over millions of years, originating from a common point out of some kind of primordial soup? Is it wise for secularists to use these theories to affirm their view that there is nothing more than time and space, the 'here and now', and that things have randomly come into being? Is it wise for us to make life decisions within this framework?

In deference to very clever scientists, my application of the three tests to the conventional wisdom about the beginning of the universe and the emergence and progression of life is at best cursory, but still enough to raise some very difficult questions for the secular expert and non-expert alike. Did you know that, as science continues its brilliant quest to understand the marvels of the universe and life, a number of once sceptical scientists are beginning to swim against the tide?

Essentially, science can only address the *how* questions, so why do many influential people rely on science to address the bigger *why* questions? Its evolution into a pseudo-philosophical school of thought, labelled by some as scientism, has profoundly affected the way we see the world as it is and ought to be. In their quest to address issues beyond their scope, do some scientists risk corrupting the scientific process, by violating the law of cause and effect and attempting to harmonise contradictory views? Is it possible that, by mistakenly elevating it to a philosophical level, people will even become disillusioned with science per se?

It is salutary to remember that pure science is neither good nor bad, only an enabler for either. I have always been fascinated by how things work and the explosive growth in technology. Just take the little Apple iPod. Today's version could store 20,000 books, in ten years it might store 20 million books, and in twenty years every movie ever made – all for a few hundred dollars. At that time we might also be able to determine our personal genetic fingerprint and disease susceptibility for a mere dollar or two. One day you might have molecular-sized 'nanobots' swimming around in your bloodstream curing disease.

On the flipside, we are all painfully aware of science's terrifying potential to enable destruction. My most vivid childhood encounter with sheer annihilation was to watch a flickering black and white film of the first mushroom cloud in the desert of Australia. We now see devastating laser bombs dropped through windows from the stratosphere.

Have we distinguished between being blinded by science and being illumined by science, perhaps by teachers wittingly or unwittingly presenting a lop-sided view? Although I value my scientific education enormously, I feel cheated by the way Darwin's theory was presented as a given by my teachers and lecturers. Never once was I encouraged and taught how to interrogate the underlying assumptions to reach my own conclusions.

This reminds me of a memorable experience in 1993, immediately after the fall of communism, when I worked with a group of budding entrepreneurs in Novocherkaask, the home of the proud Don Cossacks near the River Don. Deep in the hinterland of Russia, my only way to communicate was via a very intelligent, articulate interpreter in her late twenties. She had read English at Cambridge University and I will not forget the way she described her sheer disillusionment at discovering the many books in the Cambridge libraries she never knew existed. Her anger burned at 'the system' and teachers she had faithfully trusted for a well-rounded education.

Do you think today's physics students are receiving a more balanced view? In *A Brief History of Time*, Stephen Hawking, famed astrophysicist and Professor of Mathematics at Cambridge University, writes that today's scientists describe the universe in terms of two basic partial theories, 'the great intellectual achievements of this century': the general theory of relativity for the macro, and quantum mechanics for the micro. But he goes on to say: 'Unfortunately, however, these two theories are known to be inconsistent with each other – they cannot both be correct.'

Perhaps they are both wrong. It is also interesting to note that in 1997 Hawking made a well-publicised bet with fellow particle physicist Prof John Preskill, that 'information swallowed by a black hole is forever hidden from the outside universe and can never be revealed, even as the black hole evaporates and completely disappears'. He recently reversed his view in a talk at the *17th International Conference on General Relativity and Gravitation* in Dublin. Preskill was presented with an encyclopaedia on baseball as his reward, and said that he looked forward to Hawking's detailed paper because: 'I'll be honest – I didn't understand the talk.'

Even the far-reaching discoveries of Einstein are now under a cloud. At *Physics 2005*, a recent conference run by the Institute of Physics, Dr Michael Murphy, a Research Associate at the Institute of Astronomy, Cambridge University, announced a dramatic finding from his research into light from distant quasars. If this research is validated by further experiments, it could in turn invalidate the very foundations of modern physics. If Hawking and Einstein have got it wrong, what chance do we have?

Chance can be a dangerously misleading notion. Of course random chance could not create anything, because chance of itself is merely a way of thinking about probabilities. Furthermore, on looking back over the enormous odds I have cited below for various evolutionary events happening by chance, I am reminded of a workman on our farm who had a propensity to exaggerate. One afternoon he said he was so hungry that he ate a whole leg of lamb that had been cooked for dinner. My father's sardonic reply was 'did you have it in sandwiches?'.

I can only wonder about 'chance' when I gaze across our spring garden, blooming with sweet smelling roses and buzzing with busy bees, bathed in golden light from the late afternoon sun, as the cool of the evening settles, on schedule, once again. I can only wonder as the next crop of noisy, brightly coloured parrots arrive to be fed and chased by our little grandson. I can only wonder as I note the predictability of sunrise, and anticipate the dawn fishing expedition out on the bay, with the excitement of pulling in a couple of magnificent hefty snapper for the barbie (now I am dreaming). When I listen to the extraordinary genius of Mozart, who wrote his first symphony at the age of eight in a house around the corner from ours in London, I can only wonder about the random big bang and primordial soup.

To continue, it appears eminently reasonable to address in Chapter 4 the question of whether there might be a common source, or 'first cause', of the tangible and intangible things we experience around and within us.

The challenge

Exceptionally bright people continue to develop extraordinary theories, often subsequently validated by meticulous objective empirical research. Their theoretical speculations and methods are at times well beyond my comprehension, especially when they use mathematics to find solutions to physical questions.

A good friend of ours is a professor of aeronautics at a top American university, highly sought after to solve apparently intractable and often very expensive problems. On one occasion he was asked to investigate why rockets were blowing up a few minutes after launch, and on another, why wings were falling off fighter aircraft in mid-air. Incredibly, he solved both problems mathematically. Incidentally, the rocket manufacturer was saved from ruin, but because the solution for the fighter aircraft was so expensive, the manufacturer concluded it was cheaper to write off the occasional loss of a few million dollars.

As mentioned earlier, I draw heavily from Strobel, who through his book *The Case for a Creator* applies investigative skills and uses accessible language in a highly technical realm. He set about interviewing leading scientists in diverse fields, and found the tide is turning. I also draw on the approach taken by Joe Boot, Director of Ravi Zacharias International Ministries, Canada, in his book *A Time to Search*.

The beginning

Apparently the Big Bang theory is now widely acknowledged by leading scientists to be sound, but it raises big questions about how it came about. The current popular view, that it randomly originated from a 'quantum fluctuation of the vacuum', seems to contradict science's 'conservation laws' that determine which processes can or cannot occur in nature. Each law maintains that the total value of the quantity governed by that law, for example mass or energy, remains unchanged during physical processes. In simpler terms, what comes out must equal what went in.

Conservation laws have the broadest possible application of all laws in physics, and are considered by many scientists to be the most fundamental laws in nature. So how could the universe come into being from nothing when the conservation of energy principle says that energy can neither be created nor destroyed?

The same conservation principle has now been applied at the micro level, to the creation or annihilation of certain subatomic particles. Apparently this means that the 'baryon number' (equal to the difference between the number of particles called baryons and antibaryons) must remain the same throughout any reaction. However Keith Wanser, Professor of Physics at California State University, raises a knotty issue:

> The conservation of baryon number ensures that when particles are brought into existence from energy, they occur in equal numbers of matter/anti-matter pairs. But as far as we are able to observe, the universe appears to have an extreme dominance of matter over anti-matter, which contradicts the notion that a big bang produced the matter that we see in the universe around us.

So is this the first instance in physics where the law of conservation is not applicable? Some scientists simply say that such laws did not apply at the Big Bang, but cannot tell us why. Through grappling with this question, which strikes at the foundation of science as we know it, scientists have now come up with the idea of 'grand unified theory' (GUT), which hypothesises a process that allows for the violation of the conservation law. There are several models of GUT on the table, but with no general agreement. An even more ambitious idea is the 'theory of everything' (TOE), a theory of physics and mathematics that aims to explain and link together all known phenomena, i.e. everything.

Whatever! Let's assume that everything did start with a random big bang, so that we can move on to test the conventional wisdom that life has emerged and evolved since then.

The emergence of life

For many years, like most of us, I unquestioningly assumed that evolution within the species level – as I have tried to engineer in breeding better cattle, Arabian horses, and varieties of crops, was also the brilliant explanation for how roses, bees, parrots and grandchildren emerged from a common biological root. Then I discovered, somewhat belatedly, that a potentially crucial distinction is made between the former, known as *micro*evolution, and the latter, known as *macro*evolution.

It was also pointed out to me that by definition, evolution requires a sequence of events along a timeline, so any break defeats the idea. If we go back to the emergence of first life, we are faced with a mind-blowing transition from non-living chemicals into the building blocks of living cells, a leap in the same league as a big bang creating the universe from nothing in an instant. Michael Denton, Senior Research Fellow in the Department of Biochemistry at the University of Otago in New Zealand, writes in his book *Evolution: A Theory in Crisis*: 'We now know not only of the existence of a break between the living and the non-living world, but also that it represents the most dramatic and fundamental of all the discontinuities of nature.'

To explore how life might have emerged from the remnants of the Big Bang, we must move from zoology and dig deeper into the equally fascinating realm of chemistry. When he put forward his theory in 1871, Darwin had no idea about how life came from non-life, but he imagined an environment that might be conducive to the emergence of life. In a letter to his botanist friend Joseph Hooker, he said:

> If we could conceive in some warm little pond, with all sorts of ammonia and phosphoric salts, light, heat, electricity, etc present, that a protein compound was chemically formed ready to undergo still more complex changes ...

At that time, it was widely believed that life was spontaneously generated in decaying matter. Today, however, we have the advantage of Louis Pasteur's discovery of bacteria.

In 1928, Haldane suggested that ultraviolet light, acting on the Earth's primitive atmosphere, could have caused amino acids and sugars to concentrate in the sea and finally, given sufficient time, produce life. Then in 1953 in *Science* magazine, Dr Stanley Miller, exobiology pioneer who is now at the University of California, published results of trials where he produced amino acids through sending a spark into a mixture of methane, ammonia and hydrogen in boiling water. Forty years on, however, this noted biochemist was quoted in *Scientific American* as admitting: 'The problem of the origin of life has turned out to be much more difficult than I, or most other people, envisioned.'

Miller's work was acclaimed, but later on, Dr A E Wilder-Smith, who has three doctorates in physical organic chemistry and pharmacological sciences, said in *The Natural Sciences Know Nothing of Evolution*: 'Without exception, all Miller's amino acids are completely unsuitable for any type of spontaneous biogenesis.' Since 1980, NASA scientists have even challenged Miller's assumption that the early atmosphere was in fact composed of ammonia, methane and hydrogen, believing instead that the predominant components were water, carbon dioxide and nitrogen. Experts now consider it impossible to achieve the same results from this mixture.

Elsewhere, no other experiments have even come close to producing building blocks for the complex entities necessary for life, and what is more, if amino acids did occur in Darwin's primordial soup, they would show up as nitrogen-rich minerals in early sediments. Such deposits have not been found, and according to geochemist Jim Brooks, the nitrogen content of early organic matter is relatively low. In his book *Origins of Life* he concludes: 'From this we can be reasonably certain that there never was any substantial amount of 'primitive soup' on Earth when pre-Cambrian sediments were formed; if such a soup ever existed it was only for a brief period of time.'

Prof Stephen Meyer, whose dissertation at Cambridge University analysed scientific and methodological issues in origin-of-life biology, adds that amino acids would have readily reacted with other chemicals, creating a tremendous barrier to the formation of life. Furthermore, Prof Klaus Dose, President of the Institute of Biochemistry at the University of Johannes Gutenberg, has stated that the difficulties in synthesising DNA and RNA 'are at present beyond our imagination'.

Here is yet another quandary. Scientists agree that the presence of oxygen in the early atmosphere would prevent evolution, because it is impossible for these building blocks to arise in the presence of oxygen. But if there were no oxygen, there was no ozone layer to protect any primitive life from destruction by the sun's ultraviolet radiation. What is more, according to the second law of thermodynamics, all organic matter would actually degrade with time, acting against any evolution of primitive life.

Now we can begin to see why people like Miller have concluded that the question of the origin of life is turning out to be much more thorny than some had envisioned.

Some scientists still persist with the imaginary soup, and propose that it might produce life by leaving it alone for billions of years and relying on *random chance*. Although this idea is still the conventional wisdom at the popular level, I wonder how many punters like you and me appreciate the extraordinary number crunching done by various scientists. For example, Meyer told Strobel that the probability of a relatively short functional protein forming is one chance in a hundred thousand trillion trillion trillion trillion trillion trillion trillion trillion trillion trillion. And that a minimally complex cell requires three to five hundred protein molecules. Furthermore, all this would have to occur in a mere 100 million years between the Earth cooling and the first microfossils found.

Walter Bradley, Professor Emeritus of Mechanical Engineering, Texas A & M University, and co-author of *The Mystery of Life's Origin*, says this about the probability of creating protein molecules over time:

> If you took all the carbon in the universe and put it on the face of the Earth, allowed it to chemically react at the most rapid rate possible, and left it for a billion years, the odds of creating just one functional protein molecule would be one chance in 10 with sixty zeros after it.

Likewise, Michael Behe, Professor of Biochemistry, Department of Biological Sciences, Lehigh University in Pennsylvania, estimates that:

> The probability of linking together just one hundred amino acids to create one protein molecule by chance would be the same as a blindfolded man finding one marked grain of sand somewhere in the vastness of the Sahara Desert – and doing it not just once, but three different times.

Meyer argues that natural selection does not work at the level of chemical evolution, and claims that most origin-of-life scientists had become disenchanted with random chance and natural selection by the early 1970s. Consequently, some explored a third possibility – various theories that allow for amino acids to 'self-organise' into information-bearing DNA. But there are only some very slight affinities between amino acids, and only regular patterns like inorganic crystals could be created this way. This cannot explain the irregularity in the sequencing of DNA.

This leads to one of the most perplexing of all questions: the biological information needed to assemble the DNA and operate the system. The creation and transmission of information is fundamental to the conduct of all scientific enquiry and life itself. Each DNA molecule contains vast amounts of information, but it can never alter or add to its given information content. And a mutation (a copying mistake) only results in a loss of information. According to Bernd-Olaf Küppers, researcher at the Max Planck Institute for Biophysical Chemistry and author of *Information and the Origin of Life*: 'The problem of the origin of life is clearly basically equivalent to the problem of the origin of biological information.'

Leading information scientist Werner Gitt, retired director and professor at the German Federal Institute of Physics and Technology, says in his book, *In the Beginning Was Information*: 'There is no known natural law through which matter can give rise to information, neither is there any physical process or material phenomenon known that can do this.' This brings to mind our earlier look at the development of the physical brain and the non-physical mind. At a talk I once attended, John Lennox, Fellow in Mathematics and the Philosophy of Science at Oxford, described how he once enlivened an otherwise dry dinner conversation with an atheistic professor of physics. Although he imagined his colleague could describe the physical and chemical attributes of the ink and paper of the menu, he asked if he could do likewise about the attached meaning.

Every piece of information needs a sender and is intended for one or many recipients. Transmission requires a physical carrier and a defined code, representing ideas in the form of symbols. We convey information via a 26-letter alphabet, or the zeros and ones used in computer binary code. One of the extraordinary discoveries of the twentieth century was that DNA stores detailed instructions to assemble proteins in the form of a four-character digital code, AGCT, comprising chemicals called adenine, guanine, cytosine and thymine.

For natural selection to occur reproduction is required, and that requires cell division, which in turn requires information-rich material. To address the complexity issue of DNA, some have proposed that the much less complex RNA originated life. But the RNA still needs information to function, and for a single RNA strand to replicate, another identical RNA molecule must be nearby, which according to Meyer would require a library of ten billion billion billion billion billion billion RNA molecules.

We can conclude this section with a prescient quote by Sir Francis Crick, Nobel Prize winner and co-discoverer of DNA: 'The origin of life appears to be almost a miracle, so many are the conditions which would have to be satisfied to get it going.' I wonder how Crick might distinguish between 'almost a miracle' and 'a real miracle'.

The progression of life

Talking about the miraculous, Darwin provided secularism with the idea that every species alive or extinct today is descended from single-celled organisms giving rise to more and more complex life forms. But Darwin acknowledged his biggest problem was a lack of fossil evidence for this theory:

> Why is not every geological formation and every stratum full of such intermediate links? Geology assuredly does not reveal any such finely graded organic chain; and this perhaps is the most obvious and gravest objection which can be urged against my theory.

He looked to subsequent fossil discoveries to validate his theory, but none have been found. It seems that most, if not all, of the major groups of animals 'sprang to life' around 350 million years ago, in what is described by scientists as the Cambrian Explosion. According to palaeontologists, this occurred over a mere five million years or less, which put in perspective, would amount to one minute if the entire history of the Earth were compressed into 24 hours.

This quantum leap in biological complexity contradicts Darwinian gradualism. Darwin himself admitted that the Cambrian Explosion was 'inexplicable' and provided a 'valid argument' against his theory. A counter argument that the life forms existing before the Cambrian period were soft-bodied organisms, and hence not fossilised, has been put in doubt by fossil discoveries in Australia.

Darwin believed that a sudden appearance of a new structure would be a miracle, and if the fossil record cannot prove evolution beyond reasonable doubt, then we can - in Darwin's own words – 'rightly reject [his] whole theory'. In *Darwin's Enigma: Fossils and other Problems*, aerospace engineer Luther D Sunderland reported his interviews with five leading palaeontologists from prestigious natural history museums around the world, all with extensive fossil collections, and found that not one could offer a single example of a transitional series of fossilised organisms that would document the transformation of one basically different type to another. In *Evolution Now: A Century after Darwin*, the Marxist and evolutionist Stephen Jay Gould acknowledges that:

The absence of fossil evidence for intermediary stages between major transitions in organic design, indeed our inability, even in our imagination, to construct functional intermediates in many cases, has been a persistent and nagging problem for gradualistic accounts of evolution.

Others like Gould have proposed that there are certain times when evolution massively speeds up so that the transition happens too quickly to be preserved in the rocks. But a sudden rapid mutation rate could not explain the high level of complexity in such short a time. In addition, only mutations in the earliest development of organisms have a realistic chance of producing large-scale macro-evolutionary change. And mutations at this stage usually produce disastrous results.

In 'The Molecular Basis of Adaptation: A Critical Review of Relevant Ideas and Observations', *Annual Review of Ecology and Systematics*, geneticist John F McDonald calls this 'a great Darwinian paradox'. Apparently, the kind of large-scale beneficial mutations that macroevolution needs *do not* occur, and those not needed – the large-scale harmful and small-scale limited effect mutations – *do* occur, although infrequently. Professor Emeritus and leading evolutionary biologist at Harvard University, Ernst Mayr, in *Populations, Species and Evolution*, adds that, although the occurrence of genetic monstrosities by mutation is well substantiated, they are such evident freaks that they would have no chance of escaping elimination through natural selection.

Darwin asserted that the striking similarities between early vertebrate embryos is 'by far the strongest single class of facts' supporting his theory of common ancestry. However, in his interview with Strobel, Jonathan Wells, with a doctorate in molecular and cell biology from Berkeley and another in religious studies from Yale, destroys this notion, based on three observations about the original comparative drawings of embryos by Ernst Haeckel. First, they were deliberately faked! Second, they were a careful selection that most approximated the theory. Third, although claimed to be at the early stage of development, they were in fact later stages; the earlier stages show more marked differences. So much for scientific probity, especially seeing Haeckel was first accused of fraud in 1860, yet his drawings were still in my textbooks in the 1960s.

Wells says the enduring theory taught by evolutionists that embryos repeat their evolutionary history by passing through the adult forms of their ancestors as they develop, has been widely dismissed for many decades, because it is empirically false. One example is the gill-like structures in human embryos, supposedly indicating our aquatic roots. Strobel cites *Life* magazine in 1996 describing how human embryos grow 'something very much like gills', which is 'some of the most compelling evidence of evolution'. But Lewis Wolpert, British embryologist and Professor of Biology at University College London, along with many other specialists, says that the resemblance is only illusory.

So where do these questions leave the 'monkey to man' idea? You will remember the picture, planted in our minds at an early age, of the series of figures progressing from the crawling ape to an upright person. No research has demonstrated this process. Scientist and theologian, Marvin Lubenow, uses known skeletons and skulls in *Bones of Contention* to show that they fall into an acceptable diversity of true humans and non-humans, including the extinct southern ape *australopithecines*, which on discovery was much touted as the missing link between monkey and man, but on investigation has turned out to be uniquely different.

Henry Gee, Senior Editor of *Nature* and well-versed in palaeontology, is quoted in *Icons of Evolution* by Wells as saying that all the fossil evidence for human evolution 'between ten and five million years ago – several thousand generations of living creatures – can be fitted into a small box'.

The 98% DNA similarity between humans and apes could easily be misinterpreted, as that is where most of the anatomy characteristics reside, and the remaining 2% is genetically vast. All organic beings share a great deal of biochemical similarity; for example I am told that we share 50% of our DNA with bananas, which could explain the behaviour of some I have encountered over the years. And on a hefty point of logic, it is fallacious reasoning to conclude that because all living organisms are of the same *stuff* they must be from a common *source*.

Strobel cites a number of other fallacies that were meant to support universal ancestry, including the underlying similarities between the wing, flipper, leg and hand; the alleged *archaeopteryx* missing link between reptiles and modern birds; and the *archaeoraptor* to link dinosaurs and flying birds – one of many fraudulent 'man-made fossils'.

I would like to round off this chapter on science by taking a closer look at the questions raised by the complexity, order and beauty of things, especially noting the significance of our Earth's location.

Irreducible complexity

We can only marvel at the breathtaking sophistication and complexity of this entire system, which raises yet another problem with Darwin's theory about evolution, dubbed by Behe as 'irreducible complexity'. In his interview with Strobel, Behe explains that:

A system or device is irreducibly complex if it has a number of different components that all work together to accomplish the task of the system, and if you were to remove one of the components, the system would no longer function. An irreducibly complex system is highly unlikely to be built piece-by-piece through Darwinian processes, because the system has to be fully present in order for it to function.

Darwin himself admitted that, if any such a system were to exist, his theory would no longer hold:

> If it could be demonstrated that any complex organ existed which could not possibly have been formed by numerous, successive, slight modifications, my theory would absolutely break down.

Perhaps we need look no further than the indescribable complexity of the smallest factory imaginable. Molecular and cellular biology have made enormous advances since the nineteenth century, when the cell was a black box to Darwin, just like my laptop is to me. Strobel quotes Behe, who says 'life is actually based on molecular machines', complex and highly calibrated to control every function of the cell:

> They haul cargo from one place in the cell to another; they turn cellular switches on and off; they act as pulleys and cables; electrical machines let current flow through nerves; manufacturing machines build other machines; solar-powered machines capture the energy from light and store it in chemicals. Molecular machinery lets cells move, reproduce, and process food.

Take one of Behe's examples of a molecular machine, the flagellum that propels bacterial cells. It is a couple of microns long, and most of its length is a whip-like propeller, attached to a drive shaft operating as a universal joint. Bushing material allows the drive shaft to penetrate the bacterial wall and attach to a rotary motor, fuelled by a complex process that generates energy by a flow of acid through the bacterial membrane. The propeller can spin at an amazing 10,000 revolutions per minute, and even more staggering, in a quarter of a turn it can stop and instantly start spinning the other way at 10,000 rpm.

To cap it off, this micro-machine operates like a guided missile – sensory systems tell it when to switch on or off to guide it to food, light, or whatever it might be seeking. This looks very much like a machine of such high performance and sheer elegance that a human can only dream about inventing. It would be fascinating to have Darwin re-evaluate his theory in light of today's knowledge about the complexity of life at the cellular level; the odds of evolution producing one molecular machine, let alone the number required to operate a cell, seem inconceivable. Morcover, natural selection could only occur with systems *that are already working*.

The beauty and order of things

How could such a colossal explosion like a random big bang, which by definition would blow everything to smithereens, produce our beautiful, intricate and ordered universe, without any help? We can marvel at the beauty we can see and hear, from the roses to Mozart, and at the invisible level, there is also an uncanny degree of harmony, symmetry, and proportionality in physics.

Much has been written about the 'fine-tuning' of the universe. Apparently there might be at least thirty crucial physical or cosmological parameters that make it possible for life to exist in the universe. You can imagine a set of dials, each being precisely set, and even the tiniest deviation would have catastrophic effects. For instance, in his interview with Strobel, physicist and philosopher Robin Collins, who studied physics at the University of Texas and is now an associate professor of philosophy at Messiah College, Pennsylvania, estimates that *gravity* is fine-tuned to one part in a hundred million billion billion billion billion billion. Minute increases would crush humans, reduce the Earth to a diameter of a few feet, and even make the existence of billions of stars, including our sun, impossible.

Collins gives another example, known as the *cosmological constant*, which incidentally is much smaller than would have been estimated from first principles. It is a measure of the energy density of empty space, and its fine-tuning is crucial to our survival, i.e. one part in a hundred million billion billion billion billion billion billion. This is likened to the probability of hitting a bull's eye on the Earth less than the size of one atom, with a dart thrown from space.

But it gets even more breathtaking. Collins says that if we just combine these two parameters alone – gravity and the cosmological constant – the fine-tuning would amount to a precision of one part in a hundred million trillion trillion trillion trillion trillion, the equivalent of one atom in the entire known universe. Such a figure is impossible to comprehend, let alone the vastly smaller probability required for the entire dashboard of dials to be in sync.

There are scientists who have suggested that such numbers are theoretically possible if there are enough universes, although there would have to be trillions upon trillions of universes generated to increase the odds that the cosmological constant would come out right at least once. Collins says most of the multi-universe hypotheses are not worth considering, but the most popular theory, 'inflationary cosmology', has more credibility. Andre Linde, Russian-born cosmologist and professor of physics at Stanford University, postulated a pre-existing super-space that is likened to an infinite ocean full of dish detergent. Bubbles randomly form due to quantum fluctuation, each a new universe.

Nevertheless, Collins states the obvious that, when compared with one mere universe, this 'multi-universes generator' would have to be an extraordinary machine, requiring the right structure, mechanism, and ingredients as well. Cambridge professor of cosmology and astrophysics, Martin Rees, somewhat unenthusiastically says the multi-universe theory 'hangs on assumptions', remains speculative, and is not amenable to direct investigation.

After this brief exhilarating flight through the heavens, let's come back down to earth. Scientists have generally adhered to the Copernican Principle that there is nothing special about the Earth, and life probably abounds elsewhere in the universe. But is there a risk of conventional wisdom overtaking us? Just spare a thought about the size, complexity and location of this planet.

The Earth has the minimum mass to retain an atmosphere and the minimum size to avoid rapid heat loss. On the other hand, the bigger the planet the higher surface gravity, so at a point mountains will fracture, leaving a smooth sphere covered by water. This would result in a salt problem, because marshy areas along the coast act as evaporating areas, depositing salt that would otherwise make the sea too salty for life.

Guillermo Gonzalez and Jay Wesley Richards have gone against the tide. In their book *The Privileged Planet*, they argue that our biosphere is more like a super-organism that needs the right chemicals for life and the right planetary environment, involving complex interrelationships, a magnetic field, plate tectonics, and the carbon dioxide cycle. Geologist Peter Ward and astronomer Donald Brownlee, both professors at the University of Washington, Seattle, say that plate tectonics (only found in our solar system on the Earth) 'is the central requirement for life on a planet'. The resultant mountains and continents prevent a water world, and drive the carbon dioxide-rock cycle, which balances greenhouse gases and regulates temperature as the sun brightens slowly.

By causing earthquakes and volcanoes, plate movements cycle fragments of carbon-containing crust down into the hot softened mantle beneath the plates, and the heat releases carbon dioxide, which is vented back into the atmosphere through volcanoes. The heat comes from residual heat from the Earth's formation and radioactive decay, which also generates the Earth's magnetic field to shield us from lethal low-energy cosmic rays. Even marine algae do their bit to help keep the Earth's surface from over-heating.

Remarkably, they demonstrate that the Earth *could be located in the best place in the universe* for the requisite building blocks and low-level threats to life. Starting with our galaxy, it is of a rare type that optimises habitability. Moreover, our sun and planet are located in a safe area, Jupiter protects us from comet impacts, and Saturn and Uranus protect us from asteroids. Also, our solar system is unusually circular, made possible by Jupiter's orbit. Our moon stabilises the tilt of the Earth, increases tides to flush nutrients from land to sea, and sustains the ocean circulation that keeps higher latitudes relatively mild, a unique phenomenon in our solar system. The size of the moon relative to the Earth is critical, and its formation was the result of a rare collision.

As a lead in to the next chapter, Collins describes another intriguing feature of Earth's position in the universe as 'discoverability'. The laws of nature, he observes, seem to be arranged so that they can be discovered by beings *with our intelligence*. In Strobel's interview with Gonzalez and Richards, Richards affirms that 'the same conditions that give us a habitable planet also make our location so wonderful for scientific measurement and discovery'. We can detect the cosmic background radiation, which helped us realise that the universe had a beginning. Because of the moon's effect on the Earth's tilt and resultant polar regions, ice cores have yielded information that even includes a catalogue of all nearby supernovae.

Gonzalez built on this theme: 'What intrigued me was that the very time and place where perfect solar eclipses appear in our universe also corresponds to the one time and place where there are observers to see them.' Apparently eclipses are better observed from the earth than any other planet of our solar system, and provide scientists with much rich information. For example, discoveries include knowledge about the nature of stars, that gravity bends light – important for Einstein's general theory of relativity, and a historical record enabling astronomers to calculate the change in the Earth's rotation and correlate ancient calendars with our modern calendar system.

Make of these fascinating insights what you will, but it is interesting to ponder *why*. Some speculate that this discoverability phenomenon may be part of a bigger plan, intended to point toward 'something beyond' our limited mortal scope, that transcends time, space, energy, matter and mind, even to a designer and creator of all things. At the risk of getting ahead of myself, perhaps this is also the ultimate fixed reference point – the source of a set of life co-ordinates, physical and moral laws that we need to understand for us to make wise decisions as individuals and communities.

PART TWO

SEARCHING BEYOND THE RIP

MAKE YOURSELF a Möbius Strip from a narrow strip of paper. This is a flat two-dimensional item with two surfaces. By twisting it once and taping the ends together you create a three-dimensional loop, which only has one surface. Draw a line along the middle of the whole strip if you don't believe me.

(Although discovered in 1858 by August Möbius, famed for his contributions to mathematics and Professor of Astronomy at University of Leipzig, precedence goes to Johann Benedict Listing, Professor of Physics at Göttingen University.)

If we find it difficult to comprehend how a two-sided piece of paper can end up with only one side, can we make any sense of the quest for an integral worldview? Is there a non-physical or spiritual side to existence as well as the physical, and if so, are they separate, or one, or both separate and one?

Secularism is one-sided because it denies the existence of anything beyond the material world. In view of the brief analyses in the preceding three chapters, how do you rate the key theories underpinning the secular conventional wisdom against the simple rationality and reality tests? Many insist that there has to be more, and if so, the question becomes whether we can discover it for ourselves. Stimulated by the direction science appears to be signalling, in the following three chapters we continue our search for greater meaning and those life co-ordinates.

Have you ever imagined standing between two points on the ground at say a mile apart, and then progressively soaring vertically upwards in a rocket? Probably not, because to think about such things you need to take time out, sit on a log, and dangle a line. But if you do, the points will seem a long way apart at ground level, and as you ascend, they will get closer and closer. Logically, they will become one at infinity. Now imagine that these points signify our origin and destiny, which can be traced back to a single reference point that transcends space and time.

From our perspective, at best we might catch a glimpse of the mystery of a supernatural or spiritual realm, helped by the use of *conceptual* thinking. Therefore we will *consider* whether Something Beyond actually does exist and *imagine* what it might be like.

Furthermore, if it has certain qualities, purposes and plans, only it can and will decide whether, how, and to whom to reveal them. To do this we have to turn to theology, examine the words, and lives, of history's great teachers, and evaluate the content and reliability of related writings. This is not a bad idea, if only because these form the basis for differing versions of conventional wisdom held by billions around the world.

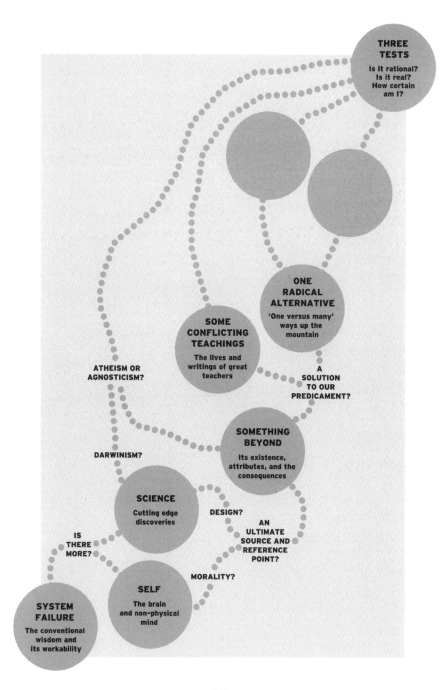

THREE
TESTS

Is it rational?
Is it real?
How certain
am I?

ONE
RADICAL
ALTERNATIVE

'One versus many'
ways up the
mountain

SOME
CONFLICTING
TEACHINGS

The lives and
writings of great
teachers

ATHEISM OR
AGNOSTICISM?

A
SOLUTION
TO OUR
PREDICAMENT?

DARWINISM?

SOMETHING
BEYOND

Its existence,
attributes, and the
consequences

SCIENCE

Cutting edge
discoveries

DESIGN?

AN
ULTIMATE
SOURCE AND
REFERENCE
POINT?

IS
THERE
MORE?

MORALITY?

SELF

The brain
and non-physical
mind

SYSTEM
FAILURE

The conventional
wisdom and
its workability

85

CHAPTER FOUR

SOMETHING BEYOND

EXPLORING WHETHER IT EXISTS, ITS ATTRIBUTES, AND THE RESULTANT CONSEQUENCES

Overview

Is it reasonable to boil down the question to Darwin versus Design? If so, we can apply the three tests to the scientific arguments and evidence for us to decide which requires a greater *degree of faith*. We either stake our life decisions on the idea that a random big bang and theories of evolution explain all we need to know about creation, or we embrace what many describe as a logical and intuitive understanding that the universe did not create itself but was designed and created in all its vastness, intricacy and beauty, by some kind of power extraordinaire, Something Beyond.

Bill Gates likens the role of DNA to that of a software programme, which obviously requires the conscious activity of very intelligent programmers. Similarly, Behe takes the simple illustration of a mousetrap: if such a lowly device requires intelligent design, what about the cell, universe, and everything in between? He concludes that science is more and more pointing to a creating Intelligence:

The conclusion of intelligent design flows naturally from the data itself - not from sacred books or sectarian belief ... The reluctance of science to embrace the conclusion of intelligent design ... has no justifiable foundation ...

Many people, including many important and well respected scientists, just don't want there to be anything beyond nature.

However, if we were to adopt the objectivity of a scientist of integrity, we should pursue each alternative, Darwin versus Design, to its logical end. Because science and philosophy cannot take us from the physical to metaphysical realm, we must journey through some challenging *theological* territory that may seem even more unfamiliar to you than the scientific material. But remember, as a fellow layman I simply want to put the right questions to the right people, including some great thinkers who have devoted their lives to pondering whether there is an ultimate point of reference, beyond space, time, matter, and energy – even something that is not only a sheer force, but also has a moral dimension, representing ultimate reality.

Incidentally, the *Oxford Dictionary* describes philosophy as 'seeking after wisdom or knowledge, especially that which deals with ultimate reality', and theology as 'rational analysis of a religious faith'. One meaning it attributes to the word religious is 'scrupulous and conscientious', essential requirements to interrogate the conventional wisdom and sadly lacking in many philosophers and theologians down through history. Hopefully such theorising will progressively become meaningful as you consider the origin of the framework from which you make practical daily choices in your professional and personal lives.

Many simply discard the notion of a spiritual realm and Something Beyond as fantasy, because it is unfathomable to the finite mind. Yet it is puzzling that at the same time they seem blasé about concepts like gravity and 'nothingness'. Have you ever closed your eyes and actually tried to conceptualise *no thing*? I have and cannot. Aristotle must have had a sense of humour to describe it as 'that which rocks dream about'. I am foolhardy enough to apply reason and imagination, through the following process, to construct a set of possible attributes that might characterise Something Beyond.

To start, by applying the cause and effect principle, it seems plausible that the 'creativity, reason and impetus' we see and exhibit could be traced back to an ultimate Intelligence. It is consistent also to apply the same logic to the existence of morality. In *Reason to Believe*, Sproul explains how Immanuel Kant concluded that to understand our innate sense of morality there must be *justice*, otherwise, why bother to be ethical? He went on to conclude that, as justice is not always fairly administered on Earth, ultimate justice must eventually prevail. Logically this could only be administered beyond the grave, by a final *perfectly just judge*. Such a judge would require perfect knowledge of all the facts and circumstances, and the power to mete out appropriate reward and punishment without being thwarted by any contrary power.

Questions now arise about the source of goodness and badness; for example, is there one power, or are there good and evil powers? Another related debate revolves around whether humanity started off in a perfect state and deteriorated from there, or whether it is evolving from imperfection to perfection. Irrespective of your conclusion to this question, if you decide that there is a Good Power, what do you think it might do about the mess we have made of its creation?

The issue of justice deserves our full attention, *because the stakes are at least theoretically of the highest order*. Let me explain. If a Good Power is responsible for a perfect moral law, as imperfect human beings we are all guilty, and due for perfect justice. We can only hope that the Good Power will not only be just, but also loving. Fortunately, love exists, and its bedfellows are mercy and grace. But unfortunately, another bedfellow of love is righteous anger, and for any law to be meaningful, the lawgiver must enforce it, directly or through appointed agents.

Now at this point, having been taken very quickly from the notion of goodness and badness to spiritual beings with person-like attributes, you are probably either thinking that my speculations are as fanciful as those of some physicists and evolutionists, or you are still curious. Nevertheless, if there is a justice issue, we are trapped in the painful dilemma faced by a spiritual being that loves its creation yet must uphold the law.

In Chapter 5 we examine the words and lives of some great teachers who might just throw some light on this problematical question, and how it might inform our decision-making.

Does Something Beyond exist?

Richard Dawkins, 1996 Humanist of the Year, Oxford University professor and 'revolutionary evolutionist', whose first book was *The Selfish Gene*, said that science's discoveries 'made it possible to be an intellectually fulfilled atheist'. Incidentally, he refuses to participate in debates with 'creationists' because by doing so he would give them the 'oxygen of respectability'. He also said: 'The universe that we observe has precisely the properties we should expect if there is, at bottom, no design, no purpose, no evil and no good, nothing but blind, pitiless indifference.'

Presumably Behe, author of *Darwin's Black Box*, uses the same evidence to reach the alternative view:

Based on the empirical evidence – which is continuing to mount – I'd agree with Cardinal Joseph Ratzinger that 'the great projects of the living creation are not products of chance and error … [They] point to a creating Reason and show us a creating Intelligence, and they do so more luminously and radiantly today than ever before'.

Taking into account these contrasting positions and the arguments outlined in preceding chapters, are you more inclined to the view of Behe or Dawkins?

How does the secular scientific view stand up when we consider the question of morality? Darwin attributes to natural selection (survival of the fittest and elimination of the weak and deformed) 'moral goodness', acting for the good of being, to bring life toward a state of bodily and mental perfection. Is he actually proposing a *doctrine* of evolution, akin to a religious belief? Many followers assume that all changes in mutations and natural selection are part of an upward spiral of progress, while others might assume that it's simply about survival. Both assumptions imply there is a goal or purpose, which again implies design, and design without a designer begs the question of intelligence. I wonder why such theorists don't assume that the changes are devolutionary or regressive, or simply deem them meaningless.

These questions suggest that evolution is not so much a question of biology as philosophy.

Those who say that the argument for design is based on ignorance ignore the advances in scientific discovery. They might discard the design hypothesis in preference to Darwinism because of their assumption that the former cannot be proved or disproved like any good scientific theory. But this assumption is flawed. You only have to take the remarkable tiny flagellum mentioned earlier; all that is needed to disprove the design hypothesis is the discovery of *one* unintelligent process to produce a flagellum, whereas to falsify Darwinism, *countless* hypotheses would need to be eliminated, one by one.

As science continues, the challenge for Darwin seems to grow. On this issue, Strobel refers to Allan Sandage, esteemed to be the greatest observational cosmologist in the world and described by the *New York Times* as the Grand Old Man of Cosmology because of his work at Mount Wilson and Palomar observatories. Sandage says that science has taken us to the First Event, but it can't take us beyond that to the First Cause. The secular view is that all we see around us came from nothing and will become nothing; but can 'nothing' produce 'something'? According to the law of causality, for there to be physical and non-physical creation, a physical law and a moral law, there must be a source, Something Beyond the forces of nature, which by definition means *super*natural.

To be consistent, though, surely an ultimate supernatural force would then have to create itself, requiring it to exist before it existed. As the concept of *self-creation* is absurd, we are left with the only alternative: this force is *self-existent* on its own power, i.e. eternal and with no cause. This does not contradict the law of causality, which says that every effect must have a cause, because the first cause, by definition, is not an effect. Those who challenge this 'first cause argument', by suggesting that logically it would be equally valid to draw the line for self-existence at the physical world, do not allow for the possibility of a metaphysical or transcendent realm, which by definition is at the highest level.

Since the birth of philosophy, great thinkers, in their ever-upward quest to find unity out of diversity, have concluded that reality needs an ultimate transcendent point of unity, the ultimate *essence* of things beyond the physical, in the metaphysical or spiritual realm. Remarkably, Alexander The Great, after studying under Aristotle, decided to translate these abstract philosophical ideas into the political, social and economic realm and create a *unified* classical culture of language, art and Greek philosophy – the basis of our modern Western culture. With such roots, it might appear strange that many now believe there is an unscaleable wall between the present and the eternal, if the latter exists at all.

Enter Kant, one of the greatest philosophers of all time. In 1781, during the Age of the Enlightenment, he published his brilliant watershed work *Critique of Pure Reason*, which seeded the foundation of today's secularism. He set out to synthesise the two mainstreams of thought that competed in the search for truth and can be traced back to Plato and his student Aristotle – logic and empirical observation, respectively.

Kant concluded that, if we can have knowledge at all, there are three requirements – our mind plus our senses plus a sophisticated system of interaction between our senses and the environment. But he distinguished between the world as it *appears* and as it *is*, and concluded that we are incapable of knowing the essence of anything, because we cannot see it in any object or person with our eyes, or with the help of the strongest microscope. So, because they are pure essence, both Something Beyond and self are simply unknowable.

What is Something Beyond like?

Whether or not you subscribe to Kant's thinking, the prospect of there still being Something Beyond is probably tantalising enough to speculate and search for clues about its possible attributes. Before dismissing such an exercise as being too far removed from day-to-day decision-making, let's employ our human faculties of reason and imagination to build a picture of what Something Beyond might be like, by extrapolating out from what we see and are, step by step.

For the dogged doubters, Einstein said 'imagination is more important than knowledge'; similarly, modern corporations recognise 'creativity' as crucial to their survival and growth. But from where do our capabilities to create, reason and take action stem?

Creativity, reason and impetus

To design and create *everything*, together with a law and impetus to maintain the running of things, suggests more of a highly creative reasoning mind in addition to some kind of physical cause or life force.

Perhaps you think the design hypothesis is flawed because of apparent flaws in the system. For example, Darwin said pollen could not have been designed because so much is wasted. But according to Richards, in his interview with Strobel, the danger in Darwin's assessment is that he might have missed the bigger picture, as he only looked at pollen from a biological standpoint. In talking about discoverability, Richards allows for a wider context by venturing the intriguing idea that pollen in lake sediments and ice cores gives us much useful data about age and ancient climate.

Also, there is the need for trade-offs in any design. Designers will agree with Henry Petroski, who in his book *Invention by Design* says:

> All design involves conflicting objectives and hence compromise, and the best designs will always be those that come up with the best compromise. One by-product of crustal plates is earthquakes that provide data otherwise difficult to obtain.

This point really hits hard as the devastation of the recent Asian tsunami, a tidal wave resulting from an earthquake, unfolded on the television screen. As mentioned earlier, earthquakes are an integral part of an incredibly complex ongoing process required to sustain life.

In business parlance, I like the term 'creation process', because it implies ongoing impetus or action, and embraces both the 'start-up' and 'sustain' phases of the creation project. At a talk I attended in 1992, Rev Dr John Polkinghorne, who worked for years as a theoretical elementary particle physicist and then a mathematical physics professor at Cambridge University, said science has discovered that, far from being a self-perpetuating mechanical process like a wound up clock left to run, 'nearly all systems of any degree of complexity are so exquisitely sensitive to the tiniest details of circumstance that their future behaviour is intrinsically unpredictable'. This is described as the butterfly effect, because the heat engine of the oceans and atmosphere that produces the weather is so sensitive that butterflies stirring the air in Africa will have consequences on London's weather patterns several weeks later.

Polkinghorne went on to say that, in addition to the familiar 'bottom-up' form of causality, in which bits of the world interact with each other, there is room scientifically for a 'top-down' causality, describing the influence of the whole upon the behaviour of the parts. If this is so, human beings and Something Beyond can continuously interact with, influence, and sustain 'a physical world that is supple and open to the future – a world of true becoming'. This is akin to 'partnership', a much espoused but highly elusive imperative for businesses battling to succeed in an imperfect, complex, global environment.

It is pertinent at this point to raise a question that dramatically polarises people. There are those that say that the world and humankind are evolving from a randomly initiated state of chaos or imperfection, toward one of order and perfection. Others say that Something Beyond created a perfect world, including its inhabitants, only for the latter to become corrupted and progressively abuse or ruin the good work ever since. You might find that the following rationale throws some light on this question.

Holiness and evil

Lewis says that logically, if goodness and badness exist and there is a source, Something Beyond must either be holy (which means 'morally and spiritually perfect, and apart from') or downright evil, or beyond both. It is interesting that people do not hesitate to use the word 'evil', but its opposite, 'holiness', has virtually disappeared from our modern lexicon.

If the good in the world emanates from a perfect Good Power, it is reasonable to suggest that there is an Evil Power sourcing all that is *not* good. Notably, many will affirm that there is a supernatural power with the capacity to influence humanity for good. But in our sophisticated scientific world it appears intellectually unacceptable to allow that there may also be a supernatural power with the capacity to influence humanity for evil. Through exploring this issue, two ideas have been advanced: 'pantheism', and the theological version of 'dualism'.

Pantheism says that everything is part of a *divine* whole, thus taking monism to another level. This is the view held by the Prussian philosopher Hegel and is found at the heart of Hinduism. But if there is a Good Power, it must be *separate* from a world where many evil things occur – a view shared by Jews, Christians and Muslims alike.

Dualism says that there are distinct good and evil powers, which are equal. But Lewis asks how this can be, when to label them as good and evil requires a third standard or rule of good, by which one conforms and the other does not. If both exist there must be a higher source of this absolute standard, the *real* Good Power.

Lewis also suggests that if dualism were true, the Evil Power must prefer evil for its own sake. But this does not reflect our perception of reality; people are not cruel for the sake of being cruel. We are cruel, either because we are sadists who gain pleasure from hurting others, or because we pursue things like money, power and safety in the wrong way. And pleasure, money, power and safety are not intrinsically good or bad things. We can be kind simply because kindness is right; but we are never cruel because cruelty is wrong, only because it is pleasant or useful.

Lewis concludes that goodness is, so to speak, just that –

goodness; badness, on the other hand, is only spoiled goodness. Which means there must be something good before it can be spoiled. Lewis says the Evil Power must have had impulses that were originally good in order to be able to pervert them; which, together with the required intelligence and will, must have come from a good creator. In other words, evil is a parasite on goodness, not an original thing, and all the enablers of evil are inherently good things – resolution, cleverness, good looks and existence itself.

If such opposing spiritual powers exist, it is also imaginable that there is some kind of battle in the spiritual realm, being all too graphically played out in the street bombings, political arena, workplace, and homes of this torn world. But if the contest is unequal, Lewis suggests it is more like a civil war or rebellion, an occupation dominated by a fierce and cunning rebel leader. For any insurgence, the rebel leader has to capture control of minds, emotions, consciences and wills. Evil planted in the human heart would then be passed on to future generations, setting in train disastrous consequences to flow down through history. We suffer the continuing effects of evil today, perhaps along with a rebel leader's persistent urging to hold on to our autonomy, for the sake of our *pride* if nothing else.

Pride, defined in the *Oxford Dictionary* as an 'unduly high opinion of one's own qualities, merits, etc; arrogant bearing or conduct', likely plays a crucial part in this rebellion scenario. Since the beginning, we know human pride has rejected authority in one way or another. History is littered with examples of tyrants, corrupted by an exaggerated sense of pride and authority, wielding power with devastating effect. So pride is an ideal vehicle through which an Evil Power might seduce us with the heady idea of taking control, and it may be at the root of his own rebellion.

Designations like 'the devil' and 'Satan' evoke an image of an absurd mythical clown in a red suit with cloven hooves, horns and a pitchfork, and should be summarily despatched along with hobgoblins and fairies. Few realise that this mocking depiction was deliberately conjured up in mediaeval times, driven by a genuine fear of the power of the evil one. It was intended to attack the one vulnerable point he was thought to have – his pride.

Ironically, if we wittingly or unwittingly reject a Good Power and join forces with an Evil Power to satisfy our need for control, we merely exchange the authority of one for another more subtle and sinister. Rather than assuming control, we are swept up in the deceptive and treacherous undertow of pride. So when we do try, we seem unable to make good and resist.

The notion of being in the clutches of an Evil Power is very hard to take, particularly for those who with pride believe they are basically good people, have got their act together, and exert considerable control over their own destiny, those who work for them, and their children. They certainly don't consciously go about their daily lives imagining they are darting from bush to bush, dressed in fatigues with pockets full of grenades, and brandishing an AK47 assault rifle. However, it is conceivable that we have operated in this manner for so long that we cannot see it for what it is.

Of course we all flippantly admit that 'to err is human' and 'nobody's perfect'. So, as none of us are spiritually or morally perfect, i.e. faultless, just how good or bad are we, and from who's perspective? And does it really matter anyway? Although those who know us would say we are not in Hitler's league, they also know we hurt others from time to time, consciously or subconsciously.

How do we honestly see ourselves? I would be surprised if you are not ashamed of many things you have thought, said and done, and not thought, said and done. I certainly am. How would you like every single thought, motive, word and action throughout your life replayed on the big screen at the Melbourne Cricket Ground on Grand Final Day? Here are some damning observations of human behaviour in *Reflections; Or Sentences and Moral Maxims* by the French classical author François Duc De La Rochefoucauld, as long ago as 1678:

> Our virtues are most frequently but vices in disguise … We should often feel ashamed of our best actions if the world could see all the motives which produced them … If we had no faults of our own, we should not take so much pleasure in noticing those in others.

In the searing presence of perfect holiness, we can only conclude that even the slightest 'fault' must be of utmost seriousness. This leads to another tough question: saddened by humanity's waywardness, would you as the Good Power walk away from the mess made of your perfect creation, or would you be angry enough to do something about it?

Justice

If this supreme Good Power wants good to prevail over evil, there has to be some kind of universal justice system to uphold its Moral Law. Even in our imperfect world we demand that everyone pays the penalty or debt incurred by breaking the laws of the land, from the petty infringement to the serious crime. Although this often comes out of the angry human desire for revenge, in our more noble moments we acknowledge that when people get away with crime, the law becomes a mockery and the weak and vulnerable are most hurt.

If a Moral Law exists, we have all broken it. Faced with the daunting prospect of receiving 'perfect justice' from a 'perfectly just judge', Lewis, who as an atheist did not like the direction this thinking was taking him, surmised that he could give up his idea of justice by putting it down to nothing but a private fancy of his own, not some independent standard. However his argument turned out to be self-defeating:

> ... in the very act of trying to prove that [Something Beyond] did not exist – in other words, that the whole of reality was senseless – I found I was forced to assume that one part of reality – namely my idea of justice – was full of sense. Consequently, atheism turns out to be too simple. If the whole universe has no meaning, we should never have found out that it has no meaning: just as, if there were no light in the universe and therefore no creatures with eyes, we should never know it was dark. Dark would be a word without meaning.

Despite what Kant might have made of this argument, for me it is enough to pursue more questions about the idea of good and evil spiritual powers. As prospective qualities of a Good Power unfold, it appears to be more than solely a mega force. Just as the wind has no mind of its own, and is neither holy nor just, a sheer force could not have such *person-like* attributes. Similarly, because a sheer force cannot conceivably have the capability to influence morality negatively, it seems consistent to assume that the Evil Power is also a person-like being.

So where does the argument take us if we now imagine that 1) the Good Power, although pure spirit, is capable of being in relationship with humans, even possibly communicating, loving and being loved, and 2) the Evil Power is capable of seducing us? The mixed emotions of love and anger in human parenting may give us some further insights.

Love and anger

Most parents say the greatest joy with their children is to experience the glorious unconditional love, freely given and received; such relationships are worth all the pain. Perhaps this is the way the Good Power saw it too, despite its probable knowledge of infallible foresight. If stuff called love really does exist, and even 'makes the world go round', the Good Power could reasonably be expected to have this additional attribute. However, some parents have been made angry enough to say that, had they known the problems ahead, they would not have had kids. After all, they only embarked on procreation for their own pleasure, but unfortunately could not produce obedient little automatons.

Love and anger are natural bedfellows. We know that love need not necessarily be soft, indulgent, or even sympathetic; tough love or controlled anger is often the only way to develop discipline. (The debate about whether discipline has any role in raising modern children is altogether another question.)

We also know that we are angered when those we love are hurt; in fact we are even angered when those we don't know suffer the terrible injustices that plague our cruel world. Likewise, a Good Power has every reason to be very angry about the way those he loves (and that includes us all) have been hurt, about our rejection of him and his law, and about the resultant mess we have created. Not plain human, vengeful, capricious anger, but a holy anger that demands nothing less than perfect justice.

(For convenience I have begun to use the masculine form of address, and hope that this does not provoke a spurious debate about the gender of person-like spiritual beings, or the misogyny of Australian men!)

Mercy, forgiveness and grace

Life on this Earth and any thereafter looks very discouraging unless the Good Power has another attribute called mercy. This must arise from a further quality called compassion. Fortunately we can imagine that compassion is also a bed-fellow of love; so, is the end of the story simply that he will *forgive* us, just like we do with each other from time to time? In fact, whether the Good Power is compassionate or not, he made us – so shouldn't he be *morally obliged* to save us from his justice?

Here is the big problem for this Good Power who hopefully desires to show perfect mercy: if he gratuitously forgives once, would he not be obliged to forgive all? Because of his perfect love for us, in part shown through his perfect law designed to protect us, he can only uphold this law by administering perfect justice to all who have hurt his creation, and that includes Hitler, you and me. Can we imagine living in a world that knows this Good Power would dismiss the genocides of history?

Many still jest that if they do happen to end up at some kind of pearly gates, they will insist on fair play by explaining that factors beyond their control, like their dreadful upbringing or inherited disposition, led them astray. Some might come cap in hand and point out that, although not perfect, 'I have mostly been good and generous, and probably more so than a lot of others in the queue'. For a boy from the bush, this evokes the image of an old stockman swinging a rickety gate back and forth as the sheep bolt expectantly down the drafting race. He decides, on balance, which are good enough to survive another day and those that will go to the knackery. This frivolous depiction of such a grim outlook is far too serious to be joked about.

Unless there is an incredibly complex merit-based formula to weigh up our performance, it appears we are all caught in a catastrophic net, faced with two prospects: not being able to meet the Good Power's absolute moral standards and not being able to engineer an escape from his perfect justice. So we have to ask him if he can release us. Whether we like it or not, he becomes our biggest fear and only hope.

If merit is not enough, there is yet another crucial attribute required of the Good Power for our escape. Although he may be loving and merciful, we still need his 'grace' to forgive us. For many, grace is probably an old-fashioned word, which literally means 'kindness, benevolence or favour freely given to those without any merit' – a rare commodity in these days of road rage and the pursuit of our pound of flesh, no matter what.

We can imagine that this attribute might occur alongside love, compassion and mercy, but even if the Good Power has this quality, he can only choose to show perfect grace once his requirement for perfect justice has been met. At this point, do you think the avenue through which this can be achieved remains an open and vexing question? Or like countless others, does the question simply not arise as you go about your daily decision-making?

The too hard basket

I have attempted to tackle some of the inevitable tough questions that arise from the above kind of analysis, but others clearly remain unanswered, particularly around the issue of evil. Why did the Evil Power decide to rebel – with such an intimate knowledge of his creator, why would he consider his way to be a better way and risk the consequences? To be able to choose autonomy, he must have been given a free will, but why? For that matter, why did the Good Power create something in the knowledge that it would turn bad, and then allow things to go so badly wrong? In fact, why didn't he discard the whole idea in the first place?

These questions are simply beyond my comprehension. You can either conclude, like many do, that they negate the concept of a transcendent Good Power, end of story, or you can put them aside as profound mysteries. I urge you to proceed for two reasons.

First, if this whole project were engineered and considered worthwhile by a supreme *creator*, who is the *creature* to argue? We can think or feel that the Good Power got it wrong, but as only he can see the big picture, any conclusion we reach that differs, must be wrong.

Secondly, the devastation caused by evil in today's world should be of the gravest concern. It would appear foolish to disregard or mock the notion of an Evil Power, in view of the hypothesis that such a being may have rebelled against his creator and seduced us all to contravene the law of the Good Power.

I have to say that those who readily seek and consider ideas for a better life, here and now, yet brush off eternal issues with a shrug really baffle me.

CHAPTER FIVE

SOME CONFLICTING TEACHINGS

COMPARING THE LIVES AND WRITINGS OF GREAT TEACHERS

Overview

History is cluttered with those who claim to have the answers to the question of justice and how it should influence our decisions in life. Most of the great historical teachers examined below have claimed to be, or been acclaimed as, messengers from God. Today there is an apparent reluctance to talk about God. Rightly or wrongly, I have not used the term up to this point to avoid all the mixed connotations and baggage that it evokes. What do you make of the advice of a good friend and successful author that the conventional wisdom says books with God in them don't sell?

This word comes from the same Saxon root as good. The original name was first introduced to the Jews as the four letter Hebrew word YHWH, meaning 'I am who I am' and 'I will be who I will be'. The Jews were also reluctant to mention the word, but probably for a very different reason. In deference to God's sheer holiness they uttered it sparingly as *yahweh*, a breath-like sound rather than a proper word. Later on it was substituted with The Lord, a familiar title for nobles and hence a more bearable utterance for the Jews. Similarly, the Muslims refer to Allah, Arabic for 'The God', with utmost respect. Is it then surprising that many followers wince when hearing the expression 'Oh my God' – one of the most widely used and trivial expressions in our Western vernacular today?

We now take a brief look at Lao Tzu, Confucius, Buddha, Hindu gurus, Moses and Muhammad, and then for reasons that hopefully will become clear, we zero in on Jesus Christ in the following chapter. Mention is also made later of contemporaries like actress Shirley MacLaine, who some consider to be the high priestess of the New Age movement (although, for many, the extraordinarily dynamic talk show hostess, Oprah Winfrey, has now assumed this mantle). MacLaine and Winfrey are in the company of countless other commentators and thinkers who believe they have additional or revamped insights worthy of inclusion in a universal framework for making life choices.

Consequently, according to the website www.adherents.com, it is estimated that there are now 1.3 billion people in this world categorised as Muslim, 900 million Hindu, 376 million Buddhist, 2.1 billion Christian, 1.1 billion atheistic or non-religious, and the rest of many other diverse persuasions.

In my view it is important to go back to the *original* teachings and the *lives* of the teachers themselves. I wonder what each would think today about subsequent embellishments and misinterpretations that their followers have allowed to creep in over the centuries. I also wonder how many gurus, ancient or contemporary, would willingly submit their personal lives to scrutiny in the light of their teaching. Because these great teachers, and their followers, have bequeathed much practical wisdom, we also touch on the *record* of much of the evidence – the great historical writings associated with them.

If you need some inducement to proceed through this chapter, let me suggest that you might discover some insights into the character of 'leadership' and how other cultures work. Many Westerners assume that their models of leadership and collaboration are superior, and often expect that everyone can meaningfully engage in one language. We have to learn more about how to co-exist in a global world, a real challenge for those deeply involved in international markets and business teams of diverse persuasions.

While students of 'comparative religion' observe common threads, the assertion that 'all religions are basically the same' shows an ignorance of the radical and real differences. At their core, clearly all are mutually exclusive. Sproul explains how our pluralistic tolerant society has mistakenly concluded that all religions are equally valid or invalid because they are rightly treated as equal legally.

Lao Tzu and Confucius

Because decisions made by the most heavily populated country are now having such a reverberating impact on the world, it seems appropriate to start with two great Chinese teachers.

Lao Tzu, born in 604BC, was an archivist for the state before he became a teacher and philosopher, living as a hermit in a mountainside hut. As the reputed founder of Taoism, initially a philosophy which centuries later became a ritualised religion, he was worshipped as a revealer of sacred texts and a saviour. Tao is the first cause of all reality, and the word means the way, truth or path. Followers believe in the unity of all things, and seek to attain harmony with the Tao, or underlying principle. Lao Tzu took a cyclical view of history, teaching that life came from non-life and returns to non-life; so true wisdom is orienting oneself to the rhythm of the universe. Five main orifices and organs of the body mirror the 'five directions', also known as the 'five parts of the sky', 'five holy mountains' or 'five elements' – water, fire, wood, metal and earth.

These rhythmic movements became characterised as the 'yin' (dark side) and 'yang' (light side). Taoism says bipolar forces –

good/evil, light/darkness, male/female – constantly react to and with one another. It also says that the true goal of humanity is to cultivate virtue, the Three Jewels of compassion, humility and moderation; but that to seek virtue shows a lack of virtue. Ch'i' is the cosmic energy or breath given to man, who must nurture and strengthen it, as practised through the martial arts. There are also several techniques to achieve immortality – described as complete harmony with the Tao – including dietary regimens, breath control and meditation, sexual disciplines, alchemy and magical talismans.

Lao Tzu is credited with writing the major Taoist text Tao Te Ching, where *tao* means way, *te* means power, and *ching* means scripture. Stanley Rosenthal, of the British School of Zen Taoism in Cardiff, has translated this work into English, and makes some interesting observations:

> It must be said of the existing English translations, that most treat the Tao Te Ching as a literary or poetic work, whilst many others treat it as a work of mysticism, rather than a work of classical scholarship, which I believe it to be, describing the key concepts of Taoist philosophy (tao chia) expressed in a poetic manner. On the matter of 'translation', I should state that I consider the term to be a misnomer when applied to an English rendering of this classical Chinese work ... I believe that any such work is at least as much, and probably more a matter of interpretation than of literal translation.
>
> ... it would seem, from historical records, that the Tao Te Ching was considered to be a perplexing book, even in the period in which it was written ... to categorically describe the Tao Te Ching as the work of Lao Tzu would be without sufficiently valid historical foundation. Even the 'biography of Lao Tzu' is not without its inconsistencies ... some

scholars maintain that the Tao Te Ching does not present a distinctive or single point of view. They argue that it is probably a compilation or anthology of sayings from various writers and schools of thought, reaching its present form in the third century BC.

It is estimated that today there are about 30 million Taoists, mostly in China, even though the communists outlawed Taoism because its passivity was interpreted as laziness, and it rejects government as an interference with the pursuit of harmony with the Tao.

The communists also outlawed Confucianism, yet it too has a significant influence on Chinese society. Confucius, born in 552BC during a time of political and social upheaval, was intent on civilising humanity, and perceived his mission as coming from Heaven. He believed in the perfectibility of humanity and focused on 'jen', understood as love, kind-heartedness and virtue. This requires loyalty to one's true nature, reciprocity, righteousness and reverence for one's ancestors. Jennifer Oldstone-Moore, in her book *Understanding Confucianism*, says:

Several celebrated sayings by Confucius show his reluctance to speculate on the spirit world and his preference to focus on the responsibility of humans in this life … he saw himself as a mediator of the wisdom of the 'sage kings' of antiquity, mostly appearing in the Five Classics, each capturing an important component of wisdom, promoting harmony and order and providing the means to self-cultivation and becoming human … Confucians hold that actions are transformative – to become an ethical person, one must be self-cultivated through the study and practice of appropriate behaviour … there is a wide range of deities and spiritual beings, which are venerated and placated at shrines and temples ... Humans who live exemplary lives may become gods ... gods are, in turn, petitioned by humans, whose offerings sustain and nourish them.

Like Taoism, the Confucian canon is almost exclusively attributed to human beings. Song philosopher Zhu Xi brought together the Four Books for Confucianism, asserting that they summed up the teaching of Confucius as touched on in the previous chapter. They became the core texts of Confucian teaching in China from 1313.

Traditionally, Confucianism, sometimes considered as a religion and at other times a philosophy, has been the basis of learning and the source of both ethical values and the social code for the Chinese. (It was introduced into Korea in 885AD, and although opposed by the communists in the north, is still influential in South Korea.)

It is worth noting that, despite severe persecution (for one vivid account see Brother Yun's book *The Heavenly Man*), Christianity is growing at a dramatic rate in today's China (understandably statistics are hard to come by, but some estimate there are now around 80-100 million followers), although the most prevalent major religion is Buddhism, which was introduced in the first century.

Buddha

Born in North India in the sixth century BC, Buddha was a prince living in luxury. But when confronted with the reality of life and universal suffering, he decided to find a solution, and became a wandering ascetic at 29. After studying the teachings of famous gurus he abandoned them all and decided to go his own way. At 35, while sitting under a tree one evening, he attained 'enlightenment' and became known as the Buddha, The Enlightened One. He spent the rest of his life teaching many from all walks of life.

When Buddha spoke for the first time about his enlightenment and resultant truths in the Hindu context, he said: 'This is the last birth. Now there is no more becoming (rebirth).'

This man did not claim to be any more than a human being, and claimed no inspiration from any external power, although centuries later he was elevated to a higher status by his followers. He said that we are our own masters, and there is no higher power sitting in judgement over our destiny. Individuals have the power to free themselves from all bondage through their own personal effort and intelligence to discover the Nirvana of safety, peace, happiness and tranquillity.

Buddha was not interested in metaphysical questions, which he saw as purely speculative, and the source of imaginary problems. When one of his disciples asked for an explanation about such things, Buddha replied that he had already explained all that he needed to – the Four Noble Truths. These are 'dukkha', the origin of dukkha, liberation from dukkha and the path to the end of dukkha. In ordinary usage, the Pali word dukkha means suffering, but according to Ven Dr W Rahula, Buddhist monk and acclaimed scholar, being the First Noble Truth it 'has a deeper philosophical meaning and connotes enormously wider senses … and so it is better to leave it untranslated'.

Three months after Buddha's death, a Council of close disciples recited all his teachings as they were remembered, and classified them into five collections to constitute the Tipitaka, or Triple Canon. These were entrusted to various elders and their successors for oral transmission to future generations in Pali, a language soft, melodious and smooth flowing. Eventually they were written down in the first century BC.

Today there is the Panchen Lama (a reincarnation of the Buddha of Boundless Light) and the Dalai Lama (a reincarnation of the Buddha of Compassion), who are both *bodhisattvas* – highly evolved beings who chose to return to our mortal world to help others find enlightenment. Despite Buddha's concern about the depressing effects of samsara (the cycle of rebirth) on the Indain people of his time, reincarnation for its ardent followers remains a central tenet of today's Buddhism.

Hindu gurus

Things get much more complicated with Hinduism, the predominant religion of the world's second most heavily populated country. This I first discovered in 1964 on a three-month trip to India with a fellow university under-graduate. We visited numerous small villages and met with government officials to explore ways young Australian post-graduates might participate in aid programmes like the American Peace Corps. Much later I read the observations of Kim Knott, Professor of Religious Studies at the University of Leeds. In her book, *Hinduism, A Very Short Introduction*, she says:

Among scholars of religion … the internal complexity of 'Hinduism' has called the term into question. Not only does it comprise the major divisions of Vaishnavism, Shaivism, and Shaktism, but it also offers a variety of different philosophical approaches, thousands of deities and their associated mythology and iconography, and innumerable ritual practices … 'Hinduism' defies our desire to define and categorise it.

We have the same difficulty in defining post-modernism; notably, an Indian recently told me that his country has always been postmodern! Nevertheless, a common feature of Hinduism continues to be the cycle of rebirth, where the self is transmigrated at death to a new body, determined by action ('karma'). Because good actions might result in a better rebirth, an ascetic lifestyle of deprivation, isolation and meditation was often chosen. It was even hoped that the cycle might be broken. However, as Knott says, because 'the suffering and inevitability inherent in the process were seen by many as intolerable', Hindu teachers offered other ways to tackle the fatalism of karma:

Krishna puts forward two innovative ideas: first, karma yoga, offering ordinary seekers the possibility of giving spiritual meaning to their everyday actions; and second, the notion that there is not one way but many ways to liberation, with seekers finding the way most suited to their temperaments and stations … Women and the low born were also recognised as seekers and invited to offer themselves, their actions, and the simple gift of water, a flower, a leaf, or fruit to Krishna … This transforms the earlier pessimistic notion – that the results of action lead to continual rebirth and transmigration of the self – into a positive discipline for personal transformation.

Many of the Hindu scriptures were orally passed down over centuries before being progressively composed in Sanskrit, and later in Tamil, Hindi and other regional languages. According to Knott:

The Vedas (hymns, mantras, spells and charms) and Upanishads (secret scriptures taught by a sage to a disciple) constitute the shruti literature and are said to have been divinely revealed; the Epics (long poems which narrate episodes in the lives of great warriors), Puranas (mythological texts often telling the stories of the gods and goddesses) and Sutras (texts about important subjects like dharma, yoga and Vedanta) are said to have been taught by sages and remembered by their disciples (smriti).

Knott observes that 'most Hindus accept the status and authority of the Veda, but very few have read it'. She also points out that, in applying scientific rigour to these texts, Western scholars are criticised for failing 'to give significance either to the role of revelation in Hindu belief or to the tradition of devotional commentary'. In fact their 'approach of critical reasoning itself distorts the meaning of scripture'.

Now let's turn our attention from the East to the Middle East, where the world's fortunes fluctuate as decisions continue to be made by political leaders about the age-old conflict between the Jews and the Arabs.

Moses

Moses stands tall amongst a number of old Jewish patriarchs, as the greatest deliverer, leader, lawgiver and prophet of Israel. He was born of a Hebrew slave around 1500BC, at the time of Pharaoh's decree that all male Hebrew children were to be killed, because of his fear of revolt. The baby's mother hid him in the reeds of the Nile, where he was found, and then raised as an Egyptian prince, by Pharaoh's daughter, who may have later assumed the throne. She named him Moses, meaning 'child', but it also means 'drawn out' (of the water). Moses occupied a position of power and received the best education, doubtless including the ability to write.

As a young man he killed an Egyptian for beating a fellow Israelite, and so had to flee the country. He spent his middle years in exile in the land of Midian, northwest Arabia, shepherding the flock of his father-in-law, an experience that held him in good stead for his future calling. One day a bush burst into flame, and a voice came from the bush, revealing that the eternal self-existent God would deliver His people. Although given miraculous signs, Moses resisted the call to lead the Israelites out of Egypt, and objected to being their spokesman because 'I am slow of speech and tongue'. He was told his brother Aaron would be his mouthpiece.

He and Aaron then went to Pharaoh to request the release of the Israelites, and Pharaoh kept changing his mind until relenting because of several devastating plagues God sent upon Egypt. Moses then led his people for forty years 'in the wilderness', and at Mt Sinai God gave him the Ten Commandments – the 'Law' by which the Jews were to live. Although a faithful leader of a complaining and rebellious people, through an act of disobedience to God, Moses had to leave it to his successor, Joshua, to take the last step into Canaan, the land promised centuries earlier to Abraham, Isaac and Jacob.

Moses is the alleged source of the first five books of the Jewish scriptures that set out God's purposes, plans, promises and laws for Jews and all the human race. Practising Jews believe that the scriptures require complete dedication. (Importantly, there are many 'non-practising' Jews of various persuasions.) The word Torah, which literally means the guidance or direction from God to his people, is applied to different collections of writings. In its most limited sense, it refers to the Pentateuch, or Five Books of Moses: Genesis, Exodus, Leviticus, Numbers and Deuteronomy. But the word can also be used to refer to the entire Jewish Bible (known to Jews as the Tanakh or Written Torah and to non-Jews as the Old Testament), or in its broadest sense, to the whole body of Jewish law and teachings.

The Oral Torah is a tradition explaining what the Torah means and how to interpret it and apply the Laws. Orthodox Jews believe God taught the Oral Torah to Moses, and he taught it to others, down to the present day. This tradition was maintained in oral form until about the second century, when the oral law was compiled and written down in a document called the Mishnah.

Over the next few centuries, additional commentaries

elaborating on the Mishnah were written down in Jerusalem and Babylon, to form the Gemara. The Gemara and the Mishnah together are known as the Talmud, completed in the fifth century. There are actually two Talmuds: the Jerusalem Talmud and the Babylonian Talmud. The latter is more comprehensive, and is the one most people refer to when they speak of The Talmud.

Throughout the Jewish scriptures there are repeated references to the promised ultimate conquering king, deliverer, priest and prophet, the Messiah, which literally means 'Anointed One'. Designations used include the seed of Abraham, son of David, Son of Man, My Son, My Servant, My Chosen One, the Branch and Prince of Peace. For many centuries this promise bound the nation of Israel together, but today there are distinct groups that hold differing views.

Most Jews deny Christ's claim to be the Messiah. A minority on the 'extreme right' still hold to the belief that a ruler will come to restore them to the land of their forefathers. Another minority on the 'extreme left' question the former interpretation of the prophets and disallow the possibility of Israel being reinstated as a political entity. The majority fall in 'the centre'. They seek to develop a higher spirituality from the old form of Judaism, and believe the advent of the Messianic age will be manifest in two simultaneous events: the final gathering of the Jewish people, and the complete regeneration of the moral world where universal peace and harmony will prevail.

Muhammad

Muhammad believed he was a messenger from God, sent to confirm previous scriptures. He accused the Jews of corrupting the scriptures and the Christians of blasphemy, because they worship a man, Christ, as the son of God. Both parties had to be brought back to the true religion preached by Abraham. Also known as

The Prophet, Muhammad led a full and colourful life, with enduring, profound effect to this day. He was born in 570AD, into a prominent family in Mecca, now in Saudi Arabia. He became a successful businessman, rejected the polytheistic and idolatrous religious traditions of Arabia and came to believe in one God, whom he called Allah.

He prayed regularly and in 610AD received the first of a series of mystical visions, or revelations, and after considerable deliberation he concluded that the archangel Gabriel was delivering God's message directly to him. As he could not read or write he asked his disciples to learn and write down his revelations, which became the Koran. Because he preached and gained converts he encountered intense opposition and fled to Medina, the 'city of the prophet'. He valiantly tried to bring peace to warring tribes in Medina, but failed, and so organised a small army to bring stability. He built a mosque and formed a government that set religious, economic, political and social rules. The Meccans attacked him; he conquered them and returned to Mecca to become the leading prophet and ruler of Arabia.

Islam (meaning 'submission' in Arabic) names more than 20 prophets, including six who are held in the highest regard: Adam, Noah, Abraham, Moses, Jesus and Muhammad, the last and greatest. However it is important to note that, in contrast to Christ, Muhammad said: 'I am but a man like you.' Islam places great emphasis on the Day of Judgement, when all will be resurrected and judged by Allah according to their works, and each person will be sent to heaven or hell. Allah only loves and will save those who adhere to the doctrines of Islam and faithfully practise the Five Pillars of Islam: The confession of faith, prayer, giving alms, fasting and the pilgrimage to Mecca.

The Koran says: 'Those whose good deeds weigh heavy in the scales shall triumph, but those whose deeds are light shall forfeit their souls and abide in Hell forever' (Sūrah 23: 107-108). Importantly, there is one way that a Muslim can avoid judgement altogether: those who die as martyrs in defence of Islam or in a holy war go directly to heaven and avoid the uncertainties of the judgement. But 'extremists' must overlook the fact that *jihad*, the term commonly used for holy war, only appears four times in the Koran, and ranges in meaning from an inward spiritual struggle to attain perfect faith to an outward material struggle. They should be mindful of these words from the Koran: 'Fight for the sake of God those that fight against you, but do not attack them first. God does not love aggressors' (Sūrah 2: 190). Nevertheless, it appears that for Muslims conquest is paramount, if necessary by the sword. By contrast, Christ said 'all who draw the sword will die by the sword' (Matthew 26: 52).

Muslims, as 'people of the book', believe that Allah revealed himself through the Torah, the Zabur (psalms of David), the Injil (gospels of Jesus), and the Koran (meaning the reciting or the reading), which supersedes all previous writings. Islam teaches that the Jews and Christians misinterpreted the Torah and Injil, now rectified in the Koran. Muslims claim that today's Koran is an exact representation of Muhammad's revelations, 'without so much as a dot or stroke ever having been lost, changed, or substituted in any way', even though it was put together after Muhammad died.

His chief successor, Abu Bakr, commissioned Zaid ibn Thabit to assemble meticulously the parts many followers had memorised and numerous fragments of existing text. While Muslims typically believe that one or more of Zaid's complete texts have survived to avoid any possible error, scholars generally agree that the oldest surviving texts cannot be dated any earlier than 150 years after Muhammad's death. Early on there were also other versions that differed somewhat from Zaid's collection.

The Sunnah is the second source of Islamic jurisprudence after the Koran. The Arabic word *sunnah* denotes the way Muhammad lived his life, so the Muslim should follow the Sunnah, although some aspects are obligatory and others are encouraged. There is also the *hadith* literature, which consists of the *narrations* of the life of Muhammad and the things approved by him, as well as his Companions and Successors to the Companions. This is further explained in Muhsin Khan's 'Introduction to Translation of Sahih Bukhari':

> Sahih Bukhari is a collection of sayings and deeds of Prophet Muhammad (pbuh), also known as the *sunnah*. The *reports* of the Prophet's sayings and deeds are called *ahadith*. Bukhari lived a couple of centuries after the Prophet's death and worked extremely hard to collect his ahadith. Each report in his collection was checked for compatibility with the Koran, and the veracity of the chain of reporters had to be painstakingly established. Bukhari's collection is recognized by the overwhelming majority of the Muslim world to be one of the most authentic collections of the Sunnah of the Prophet (pbuh).
>
> Bukhari (full name Abu Abdullah Muhammad bin Ismail bin Ibrahim bin al-Mughira al-Ja'fai) was born in 194 A.H. and died in 256 A.H. His collection of hadith is considered second to none. He spent sixteen years compiling it, and ended up with 2,602 hadith (9,082 with repetition). His criteria for acceptance into the collection were amongst the most stringent of all the scholars of ahadith.
>
> It is important to realize, however, that Bukhari's collection is not complete: there are other scholars who worked as Bukhari did and collected other authentic reports.

Although I have read an English rendition of the Koran, there is no authorised English translation. Only the original Arabic is considered by Islam to be the actual word of Allah – 'Arabic is the language of heaven'. I once facilitated a strategy workshop in Bahrain, where Arabic was the primary language for some, and English for the UK expatriates. The locals were unable to contribute on an equal footing because we were conducting the meeting in English, but when asked to put forward their ideas in their native tongue, their hesitancy was immediately transformed into animate, passionate expression.

When they then literally translated what they had said into English, we discovered how rich and colourful Arabic was in comparison. As a result the meeting became much more meaningful and productive, and I wondered how we would have managed if the boot had been on the other foot. I also wonder why a loving creator would make fluency in Arabic a pre-requisite to accessing his written word, when most cannot read this beautiful language.

Scholars note factual differences between the Koran and the Bible, and misinterpretations of the Bible in the Koran. For example, the Koran says Mary was the sister of Moses, but she was born about 1500 years later; it teaches that Christians believe that the Messiah's name is Allah, not Jesus Christ; and it says God does not love wrongdoers, yet the Bible says he loves us despite our transgressions.

In the next chapter we will investigate the teaching and life of Christ, and the trustworthiness of the Bible.

CHAPTER SIX

ONE RADICAL ALTERNATIVE

CONFRONTING THE PROPOSITION OF
'ONE VERSUS MANY' WAYS UP THE MOUNTAIN

Overview

We will now explore the possibility of an ultimate form of simplicity and clarity – a definitive reference point for all decision-making in a doubting, disillusioned world. Many people hit the buffers with sheer incredulity when one teacher in particular, namely Jesus Christ, emphatically asserted he *in himself* is the *only* solution to God's perfect justice. He said with finality that he alone is the way back to God, 'the truth' – the ultimate reference point. Out of love he also talked a lot about the dire alternative if we reject him.

This throws up the question of whether there is *one way*, or many ways up the mountain, if there is a mountain at all. In our desire for peaceful co-existence between those of different persuasions, it is reasonable to ask three questions – why would God restrict the options to one way, what kind of a God would do that, and why believe in such a narrow God? In pondering these questions, we can neither allow our emotions to override a rational assessment of the evidence, nor assume that we can have a superior view to that of God. You and I have to apply the rationality and reality tests to the best of our ability, despite opposing and often vociferous assertions made about these matters by both the ignorant and the intellectual.

Simply put, three questions seem to lie at the crux of this dilemma: is there a God and what is he like, is Christ who he appeared to be, and is the Bible a trustworthy document of antiquity?

The case for a Designer cannot be dismissed lightly, whether we have one universe or a 'multi-universes generator'. Consider Collins' assessment of the evidence as he related to Strobel:

> It's not conclusive in the sense that mathematics tells us two plus two equals four. Instead, it's a cumulative argument. The extraordinary fine-tuning of the laws and constants of nature, their beauty, their discoverability, their intelligibility – all of this combines to make the God hypothesis the most reasonable choice we have. All other theories fall short.
>
> The mission of physics is to pursue a naturalistic explanation as far as we can; but since physics can only explain one set of laws by invoking a more fundamental set of laws, it can never itself explain the most fundamental laws. Explaining these laws is where one moves from physics to metaphysics. Though invoking God may not be strictly part of science, it is in the spirit of science to follow the evidence and its implications wherever they lead us. We shouldn't shrink back from the God hypothesis if that's what the facts fit.

Or take Prof Patrick Glynn, Associate Director of the George Washington University Institute for Communitarian Policy Studies, who discarded his avowed atheism in large part due to the combined influence of his Christian wife and the extraordinary fine-tuning of the universe. In *God: The Evidence, the Reconciliation of Faith and Reason in a Post secular World* he argues that the evidence offers:

> ... as strong an indication as reason and science alone could be expected to provide that God exists ... Ironically, the picture of the universe bequeathed to us by the most advanced twentieth-century science is closer in spirit to the vision presented in the Book of Genesis than anything offered by science since Copernicus.

The Bible also makes plain that this God is a *loving* and *holy* Creator, who at the outset wrote his law on our hearts. What is more, every person has broken this law, whether a primitive native in the Amazon jungle or a civilised sophisticate in the concrete jungle, starting with the first of the Ten Commandments – 'you shall have no other gods before me' (Deuteronomy 5: 7), and stands guilty before an angry God:

> The wrath of God is being revealed from heaven against all the godlessness and wickedness of men who suppress the truth by their wickedness, since what may be known about God is plain to them, because God has made it plain to them. For since the creation of the world God's invisible qualities – his eternal power and divine nature – have been clearly seen, being understood from what has been made, so that men are without excuse.
>
> —Romans 1: 18

If the Bible accurately depicts God's attributes and purposes and man's plight, and if the reported miracles, witnesses, and prophecy show that Christ was not mistaken, mad, nor the biggest hoax in history, we are faced with a forceful case for there being only one way to live, but even more importantly, one way *to deal with the vexing question of God's justice*. To ensure that we are absolutely clear about the proposition as spelt out in the

Bible, I reiterate the story as put in a nutshell by Sproul, paraphrased along the following lines.

Just suppose that the essentially straightforward biblical account is accurate. An all-powerful God created humankind for his pleasure, and made it clear at the outset that although we could choose between submission to his will or our autonomy, the latter would have to end *in death and destruction*. Whether we like it or not, this happens to be the rule, and as a holy God he can only dispense perfect justice. Incredibly, all of us rebelled by deciding to go our own way.

However, this God also happens to be loving, merciful and gracious. He promises a way out of this terrible fix. He *condescends* to save his people, and although it is already implanted in our hearts, he spells out the law for us to follow, written down in the Ten Commandments. We still continue to disobey, but God continues to be gracious. He repeatedly sends prophets to remind us of his promise and his law.

These prophets are hated and killed, but God even cares enough to send someone he describes as his own Son, not only to mediate, but also to assume the penalty due to us, or debt we owe. God says all we have to do is accept his offer of forgiveness and eternal life, by honouring his only Son. Yet we still insist on following other people or creating alternative belief systems.

Would it be narrow-minded of God to repeat, one final time, why we should have honoured his Son alone? The Bible says this holy God is slow to anger, but we might shudder to imagine confronting him face-to-face and accounting for ourselves with words like these: 'The problem with you God is that you are not merciful enough. You are not gracious enough. You haven't done enough. Why didn't you provide more roads up the mountain?'

Significantly, God does not invite us, he *commands* us to turn back to him (technically called repentance), and to submit to

Christ. There can be no greater insult to God than to reject him and then to reject Christ, and hence no greater provocation of holy anger or wrath. I cannot help thinking that such a momentous encounter might rather dwarf contemporary debates, whether they be Dawkins savaging 'creationists', or raging showdowns between bishops and gay activists like Gary Tatchell.

In contrast to other scriptures that place their emphasis on the way to live, the Bible's central thrust is about God, his creation, the fall of the human race, and the solution to the justice question, made possible through Christ. There can be no Christ without the Bible, and vice versa. So if this document, and the claims about Christ, can withstand objective interrogation, we must be in possession of *the* word of God, end of story. This is the reason my examination of the Bible is more searching than for other 'divinely revealed scriptures'. Nevertheless, there is much we can learn from these rich and often contradictory documents of antiquity, even if only to help us understand other cultures and function better in a borderless world.

The uniqueness of Christ

Most if not all readers will acknowledge that there was a man called Jesus Christ who lived on the Earth about 2,000 years ago. Many will also say that he deserves to be another worthy contender for one of many roads up the mountain to one God. But here is the problem. He said in no uncertain terms:

> I am the way, the truth and the life. No one comes to the Father except by me.
>
> ——John 14: 6

Strangely, in our confused pluralistic world, the outrageous nature of Christ's declaration that he was born to die and clear our debt to God makes such a promise extremely compelling; a solution that Sproul says is so preposterous only a transcendent power could conceive of it. How this solution works for God is surely something we can never expect to fathom, but as with any mystery, not understanding the *how* does not necessarily invalidate the *what*. I suggest that the vast and worthy speculation devoted to the 'how' question is an unnecessary digression at this point.

Instead, in view of the nagging issue of justice, we must examine the factors claimed to support Christ's uniqueness with an open, critical mind; because if there is any chance that he is right, there are far-reaching implications. Much of the following necessarily draws on the Bible as the primary source.

His nature

Christ was clearly a radical in his day, but much more significantly, he is described as, and reportedly behaved as, two natures in one person. Although a perfect man – there is no hint to the contrary in any eyewitness account and there was no response to his challenge to prove him guilty of any wrongdoing (John 8: 46) – he experienced full humanness through tiredness, hunger, tears and anger. He confirmed that he was the Son of God (e.g. Luke 22: 70), demonstrated God's unique attributes, and *acted as only God can by forgiving people for turning away from Him* (e.g. Mark 2: 5).

We can easily baulk at this extraordinary idea, but being one person with two natures is not a contradiction. Of course it is yet another profound mystery, and those dedicated to meditation might assure us that mystery is the basis of deep and fulfilling contemplation, not necessarily despair.

His strategy

In dramatic contrast to Taoism, Confucianism, Hinduism, Buddhism, Judaism and Islam, Christ explained that *he* put in motion what had been planned from the outset – a comprehensive counter-attack to human rebellion and waywardness. Curiously, he chose not to storm into town on a big white horse, but as Lewis observes, he came 'in disguise' and called us all to join in a worldwide campaign of 'sabotage'.

I am reminded of the audacious plan of lowly Second-Lieutenant David Stirling. His idea was to drop small ill-equipped elite units behind enemy lines, relying on stealth, speed and surprise. This was a radical departure from the conventional military view that might is paramount. Through his persistence, a new Regiment was born in 1941, known as the feared SAS. Interestingly, the SAS model is frequently used today to challenge the way corporations operate and stifle radical leaders in the rapidly changing world of business. Philip Warner, in his book *The SAS*, said:

> The unique quality of David Stirling was that having devised a brilliant plan for helping to win the war he had … the drive to implement it … the gift to influence men at all levels to help him in his task … the leadership to build up morale, whether he was present or not … and, most extraordinary of all, the ability to make an apparently disastrous setback the stepping stone to a further leap forward … He took warfare several decades ahead of his time.
>
> The SAS man must always aim for the highest standards militarily, physically, intellectually, and culturally. But with it all he must always remain a modest, unassuming, ordinary person.

Although Christ adopted a relatively modest low profile 2,000 years ago, he said that he would reappear on Earth again, this time without disguise and in full force, representing God himself. At this final day of reckoning, the date of which God alone knows, all fighting will abruptly cease, the war will be over, and each of us will face the eternal consequences of our life decisions. It will then be too late to change sides; we were given an ample window of opportunity.

Crucially, Christ differed from Stirling in insisting on *non-violent* tactics prior to his return, even when up against 'the powers that be'. We commonly blame these powers, or 'the system', for seeming to conspire against us, and refer to the 'culture' or 'spirit' of an organisation. We are constantly frustrated by the inflexible and even malevolent attitude seemingly embedded in modern bureaucracies. In fact it can be similarly annoying wherever there is a hint of hierarchy, from the office, to the local golf club, church or home.

Based on his understanding of the Bible, Walter Wink, Professor of Biblical Interpretation at Auburn Theological Seminary in New York City, suggests that, as for humans, every institution, structure and system possesses a unique 'outer physical manifestation and an inner spirituality', both inextricably bound together. He surmises that 'the powers that be' make up what he calls the 'Domination System', and that 'Satan' is the 'world-encompassing spirit'. Presumably this view of 'the powers that be' would inform his evaluation of the fluctuating fortunes of corporations like Enron.

Notably, Wink leaves two questions open: 1) whether these powers are personal or impersonal entities, and 2) whether they 'possess actual metaphysical *being*', or constitute 'the 'corporate personality' or ethos of an institution or epoch, having no independent existence apart from their incarnation in a system'.

I am even hesitant to write down these ideas. Spooky images of mystical dark and manipulative forces are extremely disconcerting, so my inclination is to shy away, and fear for those who dare meddle in such things as séances with the help of 'mediums'. However, the good news must be that if all things spiritual emanate from a good God, goodness will eventually prevail over the 'fallen angels' that may inhabit institutions. If so, we are left with the questions of how, and what our role might be.

His mediation

The Bible says that Christ acts as *mediator* between God and rebellious humanity. We are very familiar with the need for an independent third party to mediate in disputes where the relationship is broken and apparently irreconcilable, whether it be management against union or husband against wife. Much of my business career has been spent in this kind of facilitative role, but only after opposing parties have been convinced that I will be able to represent both and favour neither. So who might be best equipped for this supreme role between God and us? Christ appears to be the only potential and in fact only perfect contender, because of his alleged unique dual nature.

But unlike person-to-person disputes, brokered by a third party so that each can forgive the other and move on, in this instance we have chosen to break our relationship with the supreme lawgiver, who must ensure that justice is dispensed to avoid making a mockery of the law. And what is the supreme lawgiver's penalty for breaking this law? Christ affirmed the stark pronouncement God clearly made to human beings at the beginning – death and destruction.

This evokes a howl of protest from us all, but what 'right' do we have to argue? You may have read about the distraught young Australians allegedly caught trafficking drugs in Indonesia. The most notable current case involves Schapelle Corby, found guilty and 'let off lightly' with a twenty year jail sentence instead of death. Putting aside the imperfections of any legal system, and hence the heart-wrenching question of whether Corby or the others are actually guilty, every visitor to any country is expected to know the rules and penalties, and whether they agree with them or not is irrelevant to those who prosecute their law.

His substitution

Incredibly, Christ said he took the death penalty *due to us* through God's perfect justice. A dear friend of ours is a leading judge, an impeccably just and deeply caring person. I have imagined myself standing before his stern gaze in a courtroom, having been found guilty of an offence, committed in full knowledge of the punishment laid down by the law. I try to protest before he pronounces the sentence, but he can only administer the prescribed justice. My mother dashes forward and pleads to take my place; the judge can only refuse. It seems hopeless; but then he steps down and announces that he will bear the penalty. Only he could do such a thing, because he's the judge. Would this be an act of madness, or supreme love, humility and courage?

A lasting image is the juxtaposition of two giant symbols in London's skyline. Adorning the Old Bailey is the human version of justice, Justicia, the mighty golden statue, with the scales in one hand to balance the arguments, a blindfold to show no bias, and the sword of power to punish. Only 200 metres behind, atop St Paul's cathedral, towers God's version, the almighty golden cross. The scales, blindfold, and sword are gone, because Christ cried out on the cross, 'it is finished'.

Christ endured extreme torture and a dreadful death, yet is reported to be the only person ever to rise from the dead and live forever. If he were God this could be the only outcome. After World War II, German Chancellor Adenauer looked over the debris of fallen Berlin and said that 'outside of the resurrection of Jesus Christ I know of no other hope for mankind'. Muhammad, Buddha, Aristotle, Kant and Marx *et al* died and stayed dead; the same will befall MacLaine. Incidentally, J John, an inimitable temporary Christian preacher, humorously poses this question: if you arrived at the fork in a road where there were two people, one dead and one alive, which one would you turn to for directions? I would be especially interested in listening to the one still living if he had also defied death.

Now if God did send his perfect mediator and substitute to do what he decided was necessary, there is no other who can stand in our stead to satisfy God's perfect justice. The huge difficulty for those who take this road is that, although Christ insists we love and care for people of all persuasions (because we are all made in the image of God and loved by him), we must be unswerving in our loyalty to Christ alone. This has proven to be extremely divisive throughout history, but the bottom line is not whether it is difficult or narrow or even divisive, but is it true? It is not whether it matters to us mere mortals, but whether it matters to an almighty God, if of course He exists at all.

Clearly we need to know a lot more about Christ before any thinking person will assent to and trust his claims and call. Fortunately we do not have to rely just on the teaching of Christ alone, but upon who he was and what he did.

His suffering servanthood

Christ is portrayed as the perfect man, the perfect prophet, the perfect priest and the perfect king, but also turned conventional ideas of leadership on the head by being portrayed as the *Suffering Servant*. Newton, the reformed slave trader who began to grasp the significance of the cross, wrote the moving hymn, these days mostly sung at football matches: 'Amazing grace! How sweet the sound that saved a wretch like me!'

It is easy to appreciate the difficulty a modern Chief Executive Officer might have in accepting the notions of 'wretchedness' and suffering servant leadership. But the high profile, charismatic, and heroic leadership model is under siege in our diverse, global world. Business literature is saturated with books on new ways of leadership and working together. The venerable *Harvard Business Review* has published a collection of articles in *HBR OnPoint* on *Stealth Leadership*, including 'We Don't Need Another Hero', 'Level 5 Leadership: The Triumph of Humility and Fierce Resolve', and 'Radical Change, the Quiet Way'. Research findings by the contributing authors led the *HBR* to conclude: 'Put away your charisma – the best leaders are quiet, humble, and decidedly unglamorous.'

In view of this conclusion, and another by business leadership guru Stephen Covey that '90% of all leadership values are values of character', I wonder what the inclusion of something like *Adopting a Christlike Character in Leadership* might evoke in readers. Christ appeared to show none of the attributes our secular world usually acquaints with greatness; theologian James Stewart mused that the mystery of Christ is the mystery of divine personality. Secular historian W H E Lecky, in *The History of European Morals from Augustus to Charlemaine* published in 1969, said:

> The character of Jesus has not only been the highest pattern of virtue but the strongest incentive in its practice and has exerted so deep an influence that it may be truly said that the simple record of three short years of active life has done more to regenerate and soften mankind than all of the disquisitions of philosophers and all the exhortations of moralists.

His eternal perspective

Early in my business career, a fleeting forty years ago, the company employed important and somewhat mysterious people, hidden away behind big desks in a dark, thickly carpeted inner sanctum, to make profound projections for the business twenty years into the future. I later discovered that, instead of having crystal balls, their secret was to extrapolate a straight line from past performance, which seemed to be self-fulfilling because we usually made budget. As the rate of change quickened, the horizon for many became ten and then five years. Now most companies I work with only venture three years out, although some are saying there is no point in going beyond 12 months, and others think 24 hours is a very long time. Furthermore, 'a sense of urgency' is now the catch cry, fuelled by the notions that 'time is money' and we are 'time poor'.

Compare these observations with Christ's perspective. Zacharias says that, because of his eternal perspective outside time and space (remember my earlier rocket metaphor of life's origin and destiny merging at infinity), Christ fuses every moment, past, present and future, with significance. On the other hand, the modern existentialist lives in the now, typified by the Olympic glory of the moment, while Marxist utopianism looks to the future. The Hebrew traditionalist alternatively looks to the past. *Fiddler on the Roof* recounts the expulsion of Jews from Anatevka in Russia, and as Tevye and his family move from village to village persecuted, he says they are sustained by 'Traditions, traditions. Without our traditions our lives would be as shaky as a fiddler on the roof!' With delightful sardonic Jewish humour he continues: 'You may ask, how did this tradition get started? I'll tell you ... I don't know.'

Christ repeatedly referred to the wisdom emanating from past ages, and urged us to make the most of each day. He also pointed to heaven, according to many the heart's deepest longing as poignantly expressed by G K Chesterton, a giant in many forms of British literature: 'Just think of stepping on shore, and finding it heaven, of touching a hand and finding it's God's, of breathing new air and finding it's celestial, of waking up in glory and finding it home.'

Christ also passionately and repeatedly warned against the dreadful alternative to heaven. The Bible most commonly uses the metaphor of fire for hell, and associates it with vivid words like everlasting, unquenchable and devouring. One of the most chilling biblical accounts about our prospects is Christ's parable of the rich man and the beggar:

> There was a rich man who was dressed in purple and fine linen and lived in luxury every day. At his gate was laid a beggar named Lazarus, covered with sores and longing to eat what fell from the rich man's table. Even the dogs came and licked his sores.
>
> The time came when the beggar died and the angels carried him to Abraham's side. The rich man also died and was buried. In hell, where he was in torment, he looked up and saw Abraham far away, with Lazarus by his side. So he called to him, 'Father Abraham, have pity on me and send Lazarus to dip the tip of his finger in water and cool my tongue, because I am in agony in this fire.'
>
> But Abraham replied, 'Son, remember that in your lifetime you received your good things, while Lazarus received bad things, but now he is comforted here and you are in agony. And besides all this, between us and you a great chasm has been fixed, so that those who want to go from here to you cannot, nor can anyone cross over from there to us.'
>
> He answered, 'Then I beg you, father, send Lazarus to my father's house, for I have five brothers. Let him warn them, so that they will not also come to this place of torment.'
>
> Abraham replied, 'They have Moses and the Prophets; let them listen to them.'
>
> 'No, father Abraham,' he said, 'but if someone from the dead goes to them, they will repent.'
>
> Abraham replied, 'They have Moses and the Prophets; let them listen to them.'
>
> 'No, father Abraham,' he said, 'but if someone from the dead goes to them, they will repent.'

He said to him, 'If they do not listen to Moses and the Prophets, they will not be convinced even if someone rises from the dead.'

——Luke 16: 19-31

The main point cannot be about comparative wealth because Abraham died a rich man. Instead, the story underlines the dire consequences of lack of *inclination*, not lack of *information*. Zacharias says Christ alone knew the seriousness of our plight before God.

His internal focus

When many organisations set about effecting fundamental 'culture change', they rely on the 'top-down' approach of espousing 'corporate values', although it is considered taboo to 'invade people's personal space'. But concocting and communicating corporate values to change the culture is pointless if hearts do not change. Lewis's metaphor of a fleet of ships makes the point. First, to avoid crashing into each other they need to know in which direction to travel, i.e. their destination. Secondly, they need to understand how to operate in sync. So far so good, but none of this will happen unless each vessel is in good working order. This idea became even more salient to me when I discussed with the leader of the aerobatic Red Arrows some lessons organisations might usefully learn from his team's *modus operandi*.

Christ knew that he needed to change hearts, but not by building a political power base to 'drive change' throughout the human race. Napoleon said Alexander the Great's and his kingdoms would ultimately come to nought, but Christ's kingdom is indestructible, because their way was to dominate by power and force, and his was by the power of love.

Martin Luther King, Christian reformer, and Mahatma Gandhi, a Hindu, both adopted the non-violent way of Christ with extraordinary outcomes. Gandhi once stepped from his train before a great crowd, took out a Bible, read what Christ said about humility in the beatitudes, and finished by saying 'That is my address to you. Act upon it'. Have you ever noticed that the wise tend not to be arrogant? They accumulate wisdom because of their humble realisation that the more we learn the more we need to learn.

His estimation of humanity

Christ attributed priceless value to *every* individual human being, as patiently demonstrated countless times in his life on earth. He spent much of his time in the company of those marginalised through disability, poverty, and wrongdoing, and especially rebuked his disciples for turning away children. If he is God as well as man, the significance he attaches to human beings seems staggering in the cosmic scheme of things. The biblical writer exclaims: 'When I consider your heavens, the work of your fingers, the moon and the stars, which you have set in place, what is man that you are mindful of him?' (Psalm 8: 3-4).

Moreover, by condescending to be born in our form, Christ gave supreme dignity to the human *body*, referred to by the biblical writer as the temple of the living God and to be raised again as a glorified body like Christ. This is yet another supernatural mystery, and particularly noteworthy in a society where many literally hate their bodies and in some cases starve to death as a result.

Take South African born Gregory Landsman, who through a punishing exercise and diet programme grew from a rejected scrawny kid of the wrong colour to sought-after model. Still disillusioned with himself, he resorted to alcohol and junk food, destroying all the hard work and his modelling career. He then became a make-up artist, and after some soul-searching decided to use his painful experiences to help kids with similar insecurities. In researching his book, *The Balance of Beauty Explodes the Body Myth*, he discovered that an appalling 96% of children aged between five and twelve said they were not attractive. To improve their body image, Landsman concludes that children must be convinced that their idols are merely an artistic creation, shaped by plastic surgery and airbrushed of all imperfections. He shatters the allure of those beautiful glossy magazine advertisements when he says 'a supermodel is basically a manufactured commodity … not real … a fantasy'.

His ability to inspire

For those business and political leaders who wish to inspire their followers, perhaps there is more to learn from Christ than all the current gurus put together. He has had unparalleled influence on many artists, musicians and songwriters who uplift our spirits, from Handel, Bach, Mendelssohn, the Wesleys, and Newton to 'cool' modern songwriters like the Eagles and U2.

Zacharias suggests that Christ embodied the three great pursuits of history: the light by the Hebrews, the knowledge by the Greeks, and the glory by the Romans. He concludes on this note:

> Although there are hints of truth in many other systems, the consummate expression in Christ is so geared to truthfulness in an absolute sense, that anything that contradicts it becomes false.

It is unreasonable to dismiss such musings as simply sentimental and fanciful, without examining the authenticity of this historical figure.

The authenticity of Christ

If there were a divine side to Christ's nature, we should not be surprised by supernatural evidence corroborating him as a messenger from God with divine powers. Significantly, he said to those who did not believe his words, 'at least believe on the evidence of the miracles themselves' (John 14: 11). This evidence, reported by firsthand witnesses in the Bible, comprises numerous accounts of his miracles, including his virgin birth and resurrection – both mysterious yet seemingly essential pre-requisites for him to be God. Furthermore, for hundreds of years before his birth, God, apparently in his forbearance, repeatedly sent earlier messengers to prophesy or give the human race plenty of warning about Christ's coming and purpose.

So we will now take a closer look at miracles, the biblical witnesses and prophesy, drawing heavily on the ideas of Sproul.

Miracles

What is a miracle? This became a very personal question for me as I watched my wife slowly but surely recover from almost certain death, or at best severe debilitation, after a particularly vicious assault. Hume, in *An Enquiry Concerning Human Understanding*, defines a miracle as a violation of the law of nature, and if, as he assumes, things can only happen by natural causes, then miracles are impossible. This presupposes that there is no supernatural. However, if there is a God who created the law of nature, His miracles cannot violate this law, because God cannot violate himself. So nature has to be subject to super-nature, which is not too hard to imagine; even human beings constantly work against the laws of nature, e.g. when we lift a heavy weight we do not violate the law of gravity, but simply counteract it with a stronger force.

The meaning of the word miracle has been much devalued, particularly by those Christians who ascribe it to events that are patently not miraculous. For example, strictly speaking there is nothing miraculous about the birth of a baby; it is perfectly natural. The Bible uses three descriptors for miracles that are not precise synonyms – signs, wonders, and powers. The one thing these events do have in common is the response of *astonishment*. Hence the theological definition of a miracle as 'an event in the external world caused by the immediate power of God … that is extraordinary and evokes astonishment'; something only God could do.

Although biblical miracles were used to address specific issues like sickness, they were also used to dramatise theological truths. They occurred in distinct clusters around the four epochs of biblical history, in each case primarily to authenticate key messengers sent from God – Moses, Elijah, Christ and his apostles. For example, Moses needed immense credibility to persuade Pharaoh to release the Israelites and to persuade the Israelites to follow him. More dramatic still is the bodily resurrection of Christ, validating the claim that as the Son of God he alone has the power to overcome death, the only hope for all who have broken God's law.

Christ stands or falls with the biblical account of miracles. Without miracles there is no resurrection, which means that he was just another mortal and faith in him is in vain. But many in the church still insist that the inclusion of miracles in the Bible destroys its credibility. Others have tried to reconstruct Christianity by eliminating or explaining away miracles in naturalistic terms. Some have simply decided that Christ used fraudulent techniques; it is easier to believe a cleverly conceived hoax than water actually being transformed into wine. Then in the twentieth century, scholars accepted that to take the miraculous out of these events would seriously violate the text, so proposed that the use of miracle stories was a cultural way of underlining the importance of the real historical Christ.

Another approach has been to postulate and then challenge alternative explanations, because although such explanations have staggered the mind, the miraculous is even more astonishing. Hume argues that our knowledge of miracles is based on human testimony, and our experience shows that humans can be deceived, whereas the course of nature is uniform, without exception.

Therefore it will always be *more probable* that witnesses are mistaken than nature violated. But does Hume sufficiently weigh probability as measured in the bigger context? For example, if Christ is who he claims to be, it is impossible for death to hold him, rather than it is impossible for him to be raised.

Do miracles still occur? Theoretically yes, because God's power cannot diminish over time, but if the processes of nature are the design of God, it seems reasonable that he would mostly work out his purposes through them; even in biblical times miracles were reserved for special occasions and not the norm. Notably, there is no evidence of post-biblical miracles equal to walking on water, turning water into wine, multiplying 'fishes and loaves' and raising people from the dead.

I suspect that most of today's alleged cases of miraculous physical healing are not scientifically verified. A recent documentary, screened on Australian television, showed a well-known tele-evangelist performing his healing powers, often aggressively and with great drama. Typically, no independent verification was reported. Where rigorous scientific examination has been conducted, very few cannot be explained through other means. The outstanding and commendable example of a thorough, objective analysis was conducted by the Catholic Church at Lourdes, which yielded only 64 inexplicable cases of healing out of over 100 million pilgrims who have visited over the past 130 years.

It makes more sense to consider physical healings as usually being due to God's good providence.

Witnesses

The question is not so much a matter of what can happen – a philosophical question, but what did happen – a question of history. Hume's abstract theorising about what happened 2,000 years ago must be evaluated against the witness of people who were there and saw it. So we get back to our reliance on human testimony, the basis of our legal system today and in the days of Israel.

Our knowledge of ordinary history is dependent on human testimony, so why should we give more credence to witnesses of the ordinary than the extraordinary? Naturally, the more extraordinary the event the more demanding we are about the reliability of the witnesses. We must also acknowledge that because people can be mistaken does not mean they are always mistaken. Here is how a lawyer might use the normal process to prove the credibility of the biblical witnesses:

- The biblical writers existed in a society that had the highest regard for the truth. Truth telling was one of the ten most important laws of the land, with the penalty for perjury being death. Known for its high legal and moral standards, this nation was hardly notorious for producing liars. It relied on the vow and oath, taken repeatedly by the apostolic witnesses in the New Testament (NT). Of course this does not guarantee that everyone told the truth.
- Key NT witnesses were sober and intelligent, not illiterate peasants given to superstition. One was a doctor and one perhaps the most educated person in the Palestine of his day. Of course great minds can be mistaken or dishonest.
- Witnesses should be morally upright, and the biblical writers met that test.
- The same writers were extremely accurate about historical matters, so why not be the same about the miraculous?
- Those who recorded the miracles *passionately* believed in their authenticity and significance. Rather than dismissing this as biased testimony, it in fact adds to the integrity of the accounts. Would you expect someone who witnessed such astonishing events to report them in a clinical, deadpan manner? Is a person who passionately believes what he or she says disqualified as a reliable witness? Surely this is a

necessary prerequisite to sound testimony.

- Eyewitness accounts can be erratic with events that take place quickly, but episodes after the resurrection took place over lengthy periods of time, involving several encounters, discussions and meals; they were not fleeting moments.
- There is not one word of *contemporaneous* rebuttal of Christ's miracles and resurrection. Even his enemies and the imperial powers acknowledged them, although some argued he did them 'through the power of Satan'.

Prophecy

During my visit to India as a young man, I had my fortune told because I was anxious about losing the current love of my life. I was shocked when a withered old man on the pavement started with some very accurate facts about my family and the girl in question. He then proceeded to forecast an extremely prosperous future, to be shared with none other than the one. Forty years later I can only conclude he was wrong on both counts (and for the record, I have no regrets). It never ceases to amaze me that even today there are many apparently intelligent people who cannot resist gazing into the crystal ball or reading the cards and stars. On the other hand, what is amazing about a God who elects to use prophecy as a supernatural means to affirm his plan? Only he could have the ability to foresee everything.

Dr Hugh Ross, astrophysicist and founder of Reasons to Believe, has studied the 2,500 prophecies in the Bible and concluded that about 2,000 have been fulfilled without error and the rest are still to materialise. In the Old Testament (OT) there are 332 predictions made about Christ over centuries before his time, all subsequently recorded in the NT as being fulfilled by him. It has been calculated that the probability of just eight of these happening *by chance* is one in 10^{17}, which apparently equates to picking up, at the first attempt, one marked silver coin from all the silver coins required to cover Texas to a depth of several feet. Of course many will still choose to accept this explanation over the supernatural.

Prophecy is about God pointing to Christ through the prophets in the OT, and the subsequent interpretation of the OT by Christ as recorded in the NT. The latter, testified by those whom Christ himself taught, says: 'And beginning with Moses and all the Prophets, he explained to them what was said in all the Scriptures concerning himself', and 'Then he opened their minds so they could understand the Scriptures' (Luke 24: 27 & 45).

Luke also quotes Christ as saying:

This is what I told you while I was with you: Everything must be fulfilled that is written about me in the Law of Moses, the Prophets and the Psalms ... This is what is written: The Christ will suffer and rise from the dead on the third day, and repentance and forgiveness of sins will be preached in his name to all nations, beginning at Jerusalem. You are witnesses of these things.

———Luke 24: 44-48

Five hundred years before Christ, Isaiah prophesied in the OT:

Who has believed our message and to whom has the arm of the Lord been revealed? He grew up before him like a tender shoot, and like a root out of dry ground. He had no beauty or majesty to attract us to him, nothing in his appearance that we should desire him. He was despised and rejected by men, a man of sorrows and familiar with suffering. Like one from whom men hide their faces he was despised, and we esteemed him not. Surely he took up our infirmities and carried our sorrows, yet we considered him stricken by God, smitten by him and afflicted. But he was pierced for our transgressions, he was crushed for our iniquities; the punishment that brought us peace was upon him and by his wounds we are healed. We all, like sheep, have gone astray, each of us has turned to his own way; and the Lord has laid on him the iniquity of us all.

——Isaiah 53: 3

Christ repeatedly issued a grave warning to those of his time: 'How foolish you are, and how slow of heart to believe all that the prophets have spoken!' (Luke 24: 25). He also spoke sternly to the Pharisees: 'You diligently study the Scriptures because you think that by them you possess eternal life. These are the Scriptures that testify about me, yet you refuse to come to me to have life' (John 5: 39-40). In other words, how can you search the Scriptures and miss the whole point. The Pharisees were a society of great learning and zeal for the Law. In their fanaticism, they almost deified the Law and their attitude became merely external, formal and mechanical. They laid stress not upon the righteousness of an action but upon its formal correctness. Consequently their opposition to Christ was inevitable; his manner of life and teaching was essentially a condemnation of theirs.

With the benefit of now having the NT to show us the fulfilment of these prophecies and the implications spelt out, how much more than the Pharisees must we consider these things? Is it enough to assert, even with indignation: 'I am an upright citizen. Sure, I'm not perfect, but I don't go round murdering and raping people'?

The first chapter of the NT details the human genealogy of Christ back to Abraham, reflecting the earlier prophecies that Christ would come through this line. But strangely, it can be argued that his life mirrored all that the OT account of the history of Israel symbolised. It is not unreasonable to conclude that this was meant to help the Jews, who knew their scripture and history well, to understand their global calling to tell the world of God's promise and plan. Yet most, although not all, Jews still to this day choose to reject Christ.

Muslims see Christ differently again. According to the Koran he was born of a virgin and was sinless, but it is a blasphemy to say that God is Christ the son of Mary because 'the Messiah, the son of Mary, was no more than an apostle' (Sūrah 5: 75). He did not *die* on the cross so there was no resurrection, although he did perform miracles and ascend to heaven. He was not the 'future prophet' Moses refers to in the OT; that was Muhammad, even though according to Moses he would be an Israelite, not an Arab.

Similarly, Muslims cite Christ's references in the NT to the coming Counsellor or Comforter as being Muhammad, even though the biblical context specifically identifies this to mean God's Spirit. The idea that God is in fact 'three persons in one' is seen to contradict the singularity of Allah and therefore to be blasphemous. (Interestingly, there is no Arabic word for three-in-one or threefold.) Furthermore, Allah is distant and unapproachable; aloof from any possibility of personal relationship with human beings as espoused by Christ.

Muslims, known as 'people of the book', recognise Jews and Christians as being people of the book too, although Muhammad is reported as saying that every infant is born 'on God's plan', but then his parents mistakenly make him a Jew or Christian. The Koran instructs Muslims to avoid making friends with Jews and Christians: 'believers, do not seek the friendship of the infidels and those who were given the Book before you, who have made of your religion a jest and a diversion' (Sūrah 5: 57). It also instructs Christians to maintain a low social profile and enjoy the protection of the Islamic community. However, I must say that, during my extensive travel throughout rural Iran in 1972, I was always warmly welcomed; in a similar way to the 'gentle courtesy of the East'.

At different times in history followers of Muhammad and

Christ have treated each other in appalling ways. The Muslims built mosques in Europe following the Islamic conquest, which were then converted to churches after the Christian reconquest. Waleed Aly, a member of the Islamic Council of Victoria, observed as he stood in the Mezquita, originally built as a grand mosque in southern Spain: 'Plonked unceremoniously in the centre of the mosque's prayer hall was the Coro, an ornate Renaissance cathedral. Anywhere else I would probably think it was beautiful but here it felt hopelessly out of place, exhibiting a kind of immature grandeur.'

He then visited the Haghia Sophia in Istanbul, one of the greatest Christian churches ever, which changed hands between the Christians and Muslims several times, ending up as a mosque and now a museum. He observed the changes to the original design and said 'at its heart this building is simply not a mosque … It felt so thoroughly like a church'.

Since his visits, Waleed Aly said 'I have been wondering why the pain and the animosity all this creates between people is necessary'. Indian-born Zacharias, a Christian scholar in regular contact with Muslim and Hindu scholars, rightly insists that we must not trample underfoot beliefs that others treasure, but questions what we do with conflicting truth statements. He highlights, from personal experience, some apparent inconsistencies that make meaningful dialogue with Islam difficult.

Many Muslim scholars reserve the right to challenge beliefs that are held about Christ, but no one is allowed to do the same about Muhammad. In certain cases there can be very serious consequences, as experienced by Rushdie. In 1989 Ayatollah Ruhollah Khomeini issued the famous *fatwa*: 'I inform the proud Muslim people of the world that the author of the *Satanic Verses* book which is against Islam, the Prophet and the Koran, and all involved in its publication who were aware of its content, are sentenced to death.'

Meanwhile, Muslims abolish the authority of the Bible because there is no known *original* text, even though there is also no original text for the Koran. Muslims also argue that Muhammad, the prophet to the world, did not perform miracles because he did not need to – the Koran is the miracle. But the Koran is in Arabic and cannot be translated, so many in the world are unable to perceive this miracle because they are unable to understand the language.

In view of these perceptions by Muslims of the Koran and the Bible, where do you stand in relation to these ancient documents? Have you ever wondered why we readily devour the latest 'new thinking' via the prolific writings of contemporary gurus or 'thought leaders' in business and personal development, yet leave the tomes of historical giants to gather dust on the shelves? In his *Financial Times* article, 'Me, me, me is business books' new obsession', Stefan Stern says that healthy sales figures for the former 'tell us something about the rather unhealthy and unfulfilled lives too many business people must be leading'. From my experience, many current self-help books are merely self-serving and contain one old idea, re-formulated, nicely packaged, and buried amongst several hundred pages of verbiage.

To state the obvious, you cannot know the thoughts of modern gurus until they put them into intelligible *words*. So if there is a reasonable God with a plan, and if he wants to ensure we have a record that reveals what we can understand and need to know as finite humans, is it reasonable to expect that his revelation will be put into words for us to hear and capture in some form? As television and the internet had not been invented during the eras of prophets, only the written word was available; and there are numerous scriptures that claim, or are claimed to be, the recorded word of God. A closer examination of the Bible is warranted, if for no other reason than the possible authenticity of Christ.

The trustworthiness of the Bible

How many people do you know that have actually read the Bible and can talk about it in a considered, informed manner? Thousands of Australians voted it as their third 'favourite book' in an Australian Broadcasting Commission TV poll in December 2004 (predictably behind *The Lord of the Rings* and *Pride and Prejudice*), yet most say they do not read it, and many assume that it must be 'full of contradictions'. In fact, the Bible has attracted more intense criticism and scrutiny than any other book, from people of all walks of life. Sadly, despite its enormous contribution to the very foundations of our Western world, the debate about its validity can be characterised by passion and prejudice. At one extreme are those who assert that, because the Bible is the word of God, it is self-authenticating and that's that. At the other extreme are those who resort to Biblical vandalism, through their hostile desire to destroy its credibility.

Like any thinking person, I require a more reasoned approach, applying the same objective criteria used for any document of antiquity. You will see below that linguistic and archaeological research provides comprehensive and compelling support for the biblical text and content. Here is the tough reality: if it is the revelation of a transcendent God, *the Bible cannot contain one contradiction.*

The Bible says it is *God-breathed*, but of course breathed through mouths of human authors, an idea described by Stott as double authorship. If its words are equally those of God and human beings, Stott says we must neither affirm it as God's word in such a way as to deny its human authorship nor vice versa, i.e. we must affirm both equally, refusing to allow either to contradict or even modify the other. God could have chosen to speak without smothering the personality of the human authors, and men could have used their faculties freely without distorting the truth. The same principle applies to affirming the dual God/man nature of Christ, already touched on above.

As for any old document, we must take into account the effects of cultural conditioning on both the ancient authors and modern readers, and decide whether there is an inner unchanging revelation cloaked in cultural attire – a person will wear different clothes in different situations, but we can still discern the person. Radical theologians like German Rudolf Bultmann and British John Hick were modern men seeking a modern message for a modern world, but did they accurately distinguish between the baby and the bath water? Proper interpretation requires us to consider what the author intended to say and what, if any, is the contemporary message.

The Bible also says it is *useful*, because 1) it shows the way to deal with the consequences of our rebellion, and 2) it instructs in the way God intends us to live, which is very different to the post-Christ era, as accurately depicted by the Bible in three ways – *misdirected love* – self interest instead of love for God and neighbour; *empty religion* – faith systems developed by humans compared with the 'good news' of Christ; and *the cult of an open mind* – where people listen to anybody, never arrive at the truth and nail their colours to the fence. In the words of Lewis, those who 'cannot tolerate the tyrannous noon of revelation, but far prefer the cool twilight of free thought in which nothing is true and nothing is false – you can believe whatever you like'. If tolerance is your watchword, I challenge you to read the following analysis with an open mind.

The literal meaning of the word Bible is 'The Book'. Although allegedly inspired by God, he chose to rely on human authors to do the writing, in their particular styles and languages of the time – Hebrew for the OT and Greek for the NT. Christ probably spoke Aramaic, the common language for Palestine, and perhaps Greek as well, because it was the *lingua franca* of the Greek-

Roman Empire. It is interesting to ponder why God would choose these particular languages as the vehicle for his revelation to the human race.

The Christian Bible appears to be a carefully ordered collection of books, comprising 39 in the OT (the Jewish scripture), and 27 in the NT, which captured Christ's life and teaching. For several hundred years after Christ, church councils met to determine which books should be included in the NT. During this gradual and exhaustive process a number of historical and theological criteria were consistently applied, including authorship by the immediate followers of Christ (the apostles) or their companions, complementarity with other accepted original teaching, and frequency of use by the early church. Prof Bruce Metzger, Princeton Theological Seminary, and Prof Lee McDonald, Acadia Divinity College in Nova Scotia, are among many scholars who have written comprehensively on this subject.

We can trace the origins of our Western legal system back to the Bible. Its impact on modern science and medicine has been profound, and its influence on the arts is striking – from Shakespeare to Bach. Most modern languages are heavily influenced by biblical translation, and translators, like Luther, Wycliffe, Tyndale, and Carey established many of the foundations of our modern world. Inspired by an accessible Bible, Christians built the first hospitals and schools, and led in the abolishment of the slave trade and child labour, the establishment of trade unions, provision of clean water, proper sanitation, orphanages, improved conditions for women and the mentally ill, most charitable organisations ... and so the list goes on.

Like for the Koran, many have and do put their lives at risk to defend the Bible as none other than the word of God. A great moment in history occurred when Martin Luther stood in abject humility before the might of the Catholic Church, which had put its authority over the Bible, and said he could not recant his works because 'my conscience is captive to the word of God'.

As opposed to Luther, many others have chosen to reject those things in the Bible they do not feel comfortable with. This assault on its authority, especially within the church, must be one of the biggest issues for Christians of our day, and the erosion process typically starts with fringe issues and progressively moves to the core. The 'pick 'n mix' approach looks decidedly shaky in light of what Christ said: 'I tell you the truth, until heaven and earth disappear, not the smallest letter, not the least stroke of a pen, will by any means disappear from the Law until everything is accomplished' (Matthew 5: 18). Surely such an unambiguous assertion by Christ himself, which by the way sounds remarkably similar to the assertion about the Koran made 600 years later by Muhammad, is enough to demand that we adopt an objective and rigorous approach to both books, rather than simply follow our fancies.

We must base any evaluation on legal or historical evidence because the reliability of any document of antiquity cannot be proven by scientific or empirical means. Here is a brief indication, based on Sproul's approach, of how we might apply to the Bible three objective criteria, commonly used for any historical document – the reliability of its sources, the external evidence to corroborate its content, and the kind of literature it claims to be. Sproul urges the reader to avoid the double standard of requiring one kind of evidence for the Bible and another for other documents.

Sources

The first criterion tests the authorship and surviving copies of the original. As with any documents of antiquity there are usually no original manuscripts, only copies and copies of copies. The biblical authors were mostly eyewitnesses (we have already examined their reliability) or those who seemed painstakingly to glean their information from eyewitnesses. Take Luke, a key writer in the NT, for example. Sir William Ramsey, British classical scholar and archaeologist, set out to prove that Luke was unreliable. He spent years tracing Paul's travels as recorded by Luke, and concluded: 'You may press the words of Luke in a degree beyond any other historian's and they stand the keenest scrutiny and the hardest treatment.' Modern secular historians have called Luke the finest historian of antiquity.

In marked variance to other significant old documents, the interval between NT events and their recording is remarkably short; most biblical scholars agree that the NT documents were all written before the close of the first century. The time span is also relatively short between the original writing and the earliest available copies – again less than one hundred years. Here are some comparisons:

AUTHOR	DATE WRITTEN	EARLIEST COPY	TIME SPAN (YRS)	NO. COPIES
Plato	427-347 BC	900 AD	1,200	7
Aristotle	384-322 BC	1100 AD	1,400	49
Caesar	100-44 BC	900 AD	1,000	10
New Testament	50-100 AD	150 AD	<100	5,600 (in Greek)

There are actually 14,000 NT manuscripts now available dating back to 300–400 AD, and as expected numerous copying errors appear in such a large number of documents. However, after being subjected to a vastly greater and more rigorous examination than any other old document, only serious questions about 50 passages remain, i.e. 0.01% of the total text. Furthermore, none of these deal with any major tenet of the Christian faith, and they are consistent with the rest of the text.

For the OT, following an exhaustive life-long study, fastidious scholar Dr Robert Wilson said: 'We are scientifically certain that we have substantially the same text that was in the possession of

Christ and the apostles and, so far as anybody knows, the same as that written by the original composers of the Old Testament documents.' Wilson died in 1930, prior to the discovery of the Dead Sea scrolls in 1947. Astonishingly, they contain almost every book of the OT and are dated around 200 BC.

The early scribes were scrupulous about copying biblical manuscripts. Their ritual included specially dressing for the occasion, looking at each word individually, and counting letters and lines as a check. Wilson was at least as meticulous in his comparison of biblical text with other old documents. He examined every consonant – about one and a quarter million of them – in the OT text. For example, after looking at the 195 consonants comprising the names used for 29 kings in the OT, Wilson said: 'That the Hebrew writers should have transliterated these names with such accurateness and conformity to philological principles is a wonderful proof of their thorough care and scholarship and of their access to the original sources.' He went on to say: 'That the names should have been transmitted to us through so many copyings and so many centuries in so complete a state of preservation is a phenomenon unequalled in the history of literature.'

Evidence

The second criterion draws on available archaeological and other external evidence. Interestingly, modern scientific and historical research has only added to biblical credibility. Discoveries at Qumran, Ebla, Armana, and elsewhere, have exploded the 'assured results' of negative nineteenth century criticism. Two of the eminent archaeologists of the twentieth century were forthright in their affirmation of the biblical record.

Dr Nelson Glueck said:

It may be stated categorically that no archaeological discovery has ever controverted a biblical reference. Scores of archaeological findings have been made which confirm in clear outline or exact detail historical statements in the Bible.

Prof William Albright concurred by saying that 'there can be no doubt that archaeology has confirmed the substantial historicity of the Old Testament', and made the following observation about certain NT scholarship:

> For much too long a time the course of New Testament scholarship has been dictated by theological, quasi-theological and philosophical presupposition. In far too many cases commentaries on New Testament books have neglected such basic requirements as up-to-date historical and philological analysis of the text itself. In many ways this preoccupation with theological and metaphysical interpretation is the unacknowledged child of Hegelianism. To this should be added the continuing and baleful influence of Schleiermacher and his successors on the whole treatment of historical material. The result has often been steadfast refusal to take seriously the findings of archaeological and linguistic research. We believe that there is less and less excuse for the resulting confusion in this latter half of the twentieth century.

Of course only certain aspects of the Bible can be affirmed in this manner. We can dig up monuments, but not dialogue or miracles.

Claims

The third criterion addresses the kind of literature the document itself indicates or claims to be, e.g. fictional, mythological, or historically true. The Bible certainly does not pretend to offer a good fictional read. You will see that it uses an historical style when it reports on the miracles, flood and other controversial areas, in comparison with other accounts that use mythology as a literary style. To sum up what the Bible purports to be about, Luke says at the start of his first book in the NT:

> Many have undertaken to draw up an account of the things that have been fulfilled among us, just as they were handed down to us by those who from the first were eyewitnesses and servants of the word. Therefore, since I myself have carefully investigated everything from the beginning, it seemed good also to me to write an orderly account for you, most excellent Theophilus, so that you may know the certainty of the things you have been taught.
>
> ——Luke 1: 1-4

From his subsequent text, it is clear that Luke acted as a thorough investigator, drawing on many documents and interviewing eye-witnesses to write an historical account of real events. One key eyewitness was Peter, a close disciple of Christ. Only 50 days after the resurrection, Peter is quoted as saying the following to a hos-tile audience in Jerusalem, many of whom would have witnessed the miracles and resurrection of Christ: 'Men of Israel, listen to this: Jesus of Nazareth was a man accredited by God to you by miracles, wonders and signs, which God did among you through him, as you yourselves know' (Acts 2: 22). Notably, Peter appealed to common knowledge without fear of contradiction, and in fact the first converts were made that day. Other bystanders attributed the miracles to Satan, and later rabbis claimed Jesus performed them by witchcraft, but no one said they were a hoax. This is one of the most compelling cases for the mir-acles and resurrection of Christ.

Stott emphasises that the particular literary genre adopted depends on the author's intention. He uses Luke's stories of the Prodigal Son and Good Samaritan as examples of the use of parable. Although Luke does not actually say they are parables, their structure makes it clear to ensure that no one is misled. However the whole structure and atmosphere of the account of the Magi are different; it includes references to Herod, scribes, Jerusalem, Bethlehem, the baby Jesus, Mary and Joseph. Stott insists that the burden of proof is on those who say this is not the historical account it appears to be on the face of it.

Importantly, the NT gospels had a *theological* purpose as well as an historical one. For example, John, another disciple of Jesus, selected and arranged his material to make the story logical rather than chronological. And yet another disciple, Matthew, grouped seven parables together, but did not mean to infer that Christ recited them one after the other. Luke began his account of Christ's public ministry with his rejection at Nazareth, John with his removal of traders from the temple. Such events may have occurred twice, but it is more likely that the writers rearranged the chronology for dramatic effect. If that is the authors' intention we cannot quarrel or say they are mistaken; they were simply recording the events and their experiences in their own way.

Stott refutes the idea of *limited inerrancy*, because the Bible affirms the scientific and historical as well as the theological and ethical, and where these areas appear together they cannot be disentangled. For example, 'God created the heavens and the earth' is both a theological and scientific statement; 'Christ died to save us' is both a theological and historical statement.

Another danger Stott raises is the idea of *literalistic inerrancy*. There are many instances where the biblical authors are not woodenly literalistic. God created all things in progressive stages but not necessarily in six 24-hour days. Luke said that 'all the Jews came from every nation under heaven' but then specified 15 regions around the Mediterranean basin. We need to discern when biblical writers describe things with hyperbole, poetry, or as they appear to the naked eye: by saying that the sun rises in the east and sets in the west carried no less weight then than it does now. As with any book, we must always go back to the author's perspective.

Stott says that biblical authors also used the literary conventions of their day. For instance, they rounded numbers and summarised OT text instead of repeating it verbatim. It is thus important that we do not impose today's computer-based standards of precision on biblical chronology. Publishing under another name was also a recognised and acceptable form of literature in the first century, so it is acceptable in the Bible, but only if readers could not be deceived because it was a transparent literary device. Stott notes another obvious point that some parts of the Bible are 'written better' than others, but not necessarily with any loss of meaning.

Clearly not every biblical discrepancy has been resolved, but as scholarship develops and knowledge of language, text and context increases, the problem of discrepancy becomes smaller and smaller. From my personal experience, the assertion that 'the Bible is full of contradictions' is invariably rash and the result of sheer ignorance. Some fall for the simple trap of thinking that variant accounts are the same as contradictory accounts. Take an obvious example; if a writer recorded one figure at an event and another reported two, there would only be a contradiction if the former had said there was *only* one present.

Perhaps most importantly, all questions have to be put in the bigger context, by looking at the whole thrust of scripture, which has a clear unity and cohesion, albeit with differing theological emphases. Stott says we should not try 'to iron out these creases' and lose the richness. Christ too implies that some elements are weightier than others. Finally, like for any other document, we should avoid the temptation of 'random dipping' to seek guidance or prove a point, and we should never try to align the whole Bible with our interpretation of a particular text, but rather interrogate the piece against the whole.

Much hinges on the Bible. After applying the three criteria to examine its credibility, i.e. its sources, evidence and claims, we can take another step by following a *linear* argument through induction and deduction, as again inspired by Sproul:

1. The Bible is a basically reliable historical document	Linguistic and archaeological research provides compelling evidence. (If this premise is not true, we have scant reliable information about Christ.)
2. Christ is the Son of God	The biblical eyewitness accounts of his life, miracles, resurrection and fulfilled prophecy are consistent in authenticating his claim to be God's Son.
3. Christ is an infallible authority	He said he taught the truth, and if he were a perfect man he had to be a morally infallible teacher.
4. Christ says the Bible is God's word	He explicitly or implicitly endorses the OT 162 times in the NT, and those he entrusted with God's final revelation wrote the NT.
5. The Bible is infallible	For God to be God he must be infallible.

Yet can the Bible still be infallible when mediated by fallible humans? The notion of infallibility has generated much heated debate over the centuries, but the obvious qualification is that scripture is the infallible word of God as originally given in Hebrew or Greek through the original authors. Some ridicule this statement because the very first texts do not exist, to our knowledge, and all known manuscripts are copies and translations. Stott says it would be wiser to accept the obvious, recognise that we need the double discipline of sound textual criticism to authenticate the text, and sound literary and historical criticism to discover what scripture affirms, conducting our study in humility rather than arrogance.

The *Chicago Declaration*, by the International Council on Biblical Inerrancy, offers the following clarification: 'Scripture is to be believed as God's instruction *in all that it affirms*, it is to be obeyed as God's command *in all that it requires*, and it is to be embraced as God's promise *in all that it pledges*.' To Stott this is a very important clarification, because scripture neither condones all that it records, nor every interpretation of its contents. Sure-handedness is required to apply the basic principle of literary interpretation so that the author's intended meaning is not distorted or misconstrued.

Having reviewed the direction in which the above analysis is pointing, I am reminded of Chesterton's warning that 'the purpose of opening the mind, as of opening the mouth, is to shut it again on something solid', even if that leads us inexorably to the prospect that there may only be one way up the mountain, if of course there is a mountain at all.

Admittedly, the line of argument leading to 'one way' involves induction or deduction by fallible human beings, premise by premise. At best, it is meant to be a process of careful historical, empirical investigation, together with logical inferences, avoiding any giant subjective leaps of blind faith. Someone once said that there are many *logic* pathways to the Truth, but only *one path* to the Truth, namely Christ.

Zacharias adds that 'a worldview is not complete in itself until it is able to refute, implicitly or explicitly, contrary worldviews'. The worldview according to Christ appears to meet this criterion too.

Right now you could just be thinking that I have deliberately and even deviously led you along a winding path with the hidden agenda of 'selling you the Christian religion'. If so, you misunderstand. Let me slightly pre-empt my personal position, as spelt out in the Postscript.

First, why would I want to sell you one religion, when like you I have grown up in a pluralist world, where so-called tolerance has been embedded in my psyche and 'religion' is *passé*? Instead, because I like to think I am a bit of a radical in search for simplicity, I need to decide whether Christ was the ultimate radical or deluded. French theologian Jacques Ellul, in *The Subversion of Christianity*, takes us back to the beginning:

> For the Romans nascent Christianity was not at all a new religion. It was 'anti-religion'. This view was well founded. What the first Christians were putting on trial was not just the imperial religion, as is often said, but every religion in the known world.

So if Christ is the only way, a religious label like Christ-*ianity* is too limiting. Potentially it reduces the Truth to just another code or religion, defined in the *Oxford Dictionary* as 'a particular system of faith and worship'.

Furthermore, categorising Christ's way as another religion has allowed for its intentional or unintentional corruption by 'Christians' and 'The Church', as so catastrophically played out over hundreds of years. In the past century, many have seen it as the thin edge of the wedge for their colonisation by Western culture, and so strongly resisted the missionary movement. In his book, *The Christ of the Indian Road*, American-born missionary E Stanley Jones recounts many examples where this resistance melted away when Christ himself was accurately represented to Hindus within their cultural setting. After all, Christ was not born as an all-white American or European. A thoughtful Hindu, obviously deeply upset by British occupation, said to Jones one day: 'If you call one of us a [Christ-like] man, he is complimented, but if you call him a Christian, he is insulted.'

At the beginning of this century, the violent reaction to today's incursions by Western powers is at least partly explained by the continuing perception in the Arab states that Christianity is the prevailing religion of the invaders. How mistaken they are. In contemporary secular Australia, a study conducted by Market Access & Consulting Research reports that, while respondents were critical of the church's adherents, they were not of its founder:

> As soon as people think of Christianity they think of Christian churches, the practice of religion and the negative associations they have with churches and their hierarchies … Jesus himself was to a large degree separated from all of these things and tended not to necessarily evoke these powerfully negative associations.

It mystifies me why people ditch Christ because of the man-made failings in the church of Christianity; my passion for my footy team has not diminished because of some recent bad management at the club. Yet I do not discount the pain of those who, understandably bemused, disillusioned or hurt by the church, are formulating and experimenting with numerous alternative approaches, lifestyles and belief systems to inform their decisions. Before we go there (in Chapter 8), we should first consider some potential implications of adopting Christ's way in our decision-making.

PART THREE

DEFEATING
THE RIP

IN 1859, THE FAMOUS French tight-rope walker and acrobat Jean François Gravelet, alias Blondin, stretched a wire rope across the top of Niagara Falls, walked it several times, blindfold, and on stilts – he even sat midway eating an omelette. Apparently he asked a reporter if he thought he could push a man across in a wheelbarrow. 'I really believe you can ... I think you are the greatest stunt artist of all time' was the eager reply. 'Well then, you get in the wheelbarrow!' said Blondin. There is a big difference between *believing* in someone and *trusting* that person with your life.

This distinction is clear when we understand how Martin Luther, the great sixteenth century scholar and reformer, unpacked the meaning of faith. Obviously, before being persuaded of anything, we need knowledge. We apply our reasoning to evaluate that knowledge, with the outcome being either assent or disbelief – yes it does, or no it does not make sense. If it does, we can decide whether to commit or put our trust in the idea, which leads to the third point on the triangle.

It is legitimate to connect this point back to the start, because only by trying can we really know. In sitting on a chair we instinctively go through this process – has it got enough legs, will it take my weight, etc; but we must sit on it to affirm our knowledge and reasoning. So the triangle is more like a virtuous circle, requiring 'active trust'.

This model suggests a linear progression, but I suspect the process is more fluid, partially influenced by our personality. Some are more inclined to lead with the head whilst others are more heart-driven. But all of us have both, and need to keep them in sync if we are to avoid a headache.

In fact, steps of faith in life can be likened more to an upward virtuous spiral, where our experience not only affirms, but also expands, our knowledge and enhances our reasoning. In contrast with our obsessive desire 'to see in order to believe', the ancient theologian Augustine once said 'I believe in order to understand'. In a similar vein, an old Chinese proverb reads:

Tell me … I forget
Show me … I remember
Involve me … I understand

It goes without saying that to entrust one's life to a particular worldview deserves much deeper thought than deciding whether or not a chair is safe to sit on, especially in view of the mess our world is in. Having closely experienced two court cases where people took very seriously the fate of others, I wonder why many do not apply the same rigour to decide the 'verdict' for their own lives.

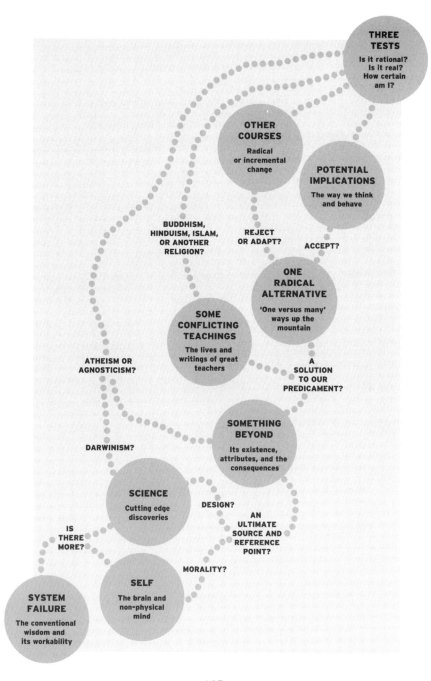

THREE TESTS

Is it rational?
Is it real?
How certain am I?

OTHER COURSES

Radical or incremental change

POTENTIAL IMPLICATIONS

The way we think and behave

BUDDHISM, HINDUISM, ISLAM, OR ANOTHER RELIGION?

REJECT OR ADAPT?

ACCEPT?

ONE RADICAL ALTERNATIVE

'One versus many' ways up the mountain

SOME CONFLICTING TEACHINGS

The lives and writings of great teachers

ATHEISM OR AGNOSTICISM?

A SOLUTION TO OUR PREDICAMENT?

SOMETHING BEYOND

Its existence, attributes, and the consequences

DARWINISM?

SCIENCE

Cutting edge discoveries

DESIGN?

AN ULTIMATE SOURCE AND REFERENCE POINT?

IS THERE MORE?

MORALITY?

SYSTEM FAILURE

The conventional wisdom and its workability

SELF

The brain and non-physical mind

165

We have already covered much of the territory in this mini-journey of words, where I have tried to challenge the conventional wisdom and demonstrate clear thinking, step by step. In the first two parts, issues raised by secularism, nagging impulses within our inner self, and developments in science, appeared to point to Something Beyond. So we considered the likelihood of a spiritual being actually existing outside the confines of our understanding, imagined what it might be like, and looked at what this could mean as a reference point for decision-making in our torn world.

Because this perhaps unexpectedly pointed to the centrality of the justice question, we sought further insights from some of the prevailing worldviews originating with several great historical teachers, with particular focus on Christ – a seemingly radical alternative.

Now we move to the third and final part, to consider some potential implications if there is only one way, and several other alternatives adopted by people who consider this to be a misguided, narrow and limiting perspective, unworthy of their faith. You are then invited to apply three tests to the various scenarios outlined.

CHAPTER SEVEN

POTENTIAL IMPLICATIONS

CHANGING THE WAY WE THINK AND BEHAVE
AS WE MAKE DECISIONS

There is a pertinent saying in academia that 'nothing is as practical as a good theory'. My daughter would also argue, as she undergoes the PhD process, that there's a real trap in theories with no practical application – the risk is all talk and no action!

When we talk of there being Something Beyond, it is all too easy to discuss and understand the corresponding matters of spirituality and yet fail to apply them, or even acknowledge their relevance, to our lives. In looking back on the last chapter, how do the arguments and observations about Christ help us to make *practical* wise decisions, both in our professional and personal lives? Accordingly, what do you make of the following implications for the way we think and behave that seem to flow from Christ's promise of eternal reconciliation with God?

Recognise the seriousness of our predicament

When certain of our behaviours are challenged, we often retort that no one is being hurt, but how can we be sure that there is no victim? On his deathbed, Arthur Ashe, the famous tennis player who innocently contracted AIDS, said that he had lived with a lot of pain, but nothing had hurt him more than the rejection of his race.

This reminds me of the familiar story of a family friend – a delightful Serbian refugee, evacuated to London eight years ago because of injury. He diligently learnt the language, went to various skills training programmes, and sought a reasonable permanent job without success. Duped by greedy casual employers, and spurned by those of his own who have been more fortunate, he is told he can only 'wash dishes' despite his previous profession as an accomplished jet engine mechanic. The UK benefits system only keeps him fed and sheltered; he has no money to socialise and meet others, or busy himself with a hobby. He has lost all hope in the fine city of London, and the prospect of returning to a home devastated by war and where his fellow Serbs continue to suffer severe discrimination is even grimmer.

But now for another telling question: how often do you think about the potential damage we do to *ourselves* when we hurt others? 'Terrible as what the world did to me, what I did to myself was far more terrible still' were the underlined words of Oscar Wilde's *De Profundis* found by former Japanese Prime Minister Konoye's deathbed. He was guilty of atrocious war crimes during the Second World War.

In our messed up world you might reasonably conclude that we urgently need to rediscover the concept of wrongdoing and its impact on others and ourselves, and ultimately on God – let alone the impact on his supposed gift of creation, designed for our pleasure and entrusted to our custodianship. We simply cannot deny the error of our ways as long as so many are being hurt around us. Even in our schools we are now installing welfare officers to combat bullying and parental intimidation.

I have already broken my writer friend's rule in using the word GOD, and now I will probably contravene the ultimate rule with the use of that little word SIN. I wonder if beneath our supercilious use of this term, or palpable reluctance even to utter it, we grasp the original Hebrew and Greek meaning: 'a falling away from, missing the right path, missing the mark, act of rebellion, violation of divine law'.

Another victim of suicide, psychologist O Hobart Mowrer

(pioneer of 'integrity therapy' that led to 'reality therapy', and one-time president of the American Psychological Association) wrote an article in 1960 that reportedly generated more mail than anything else he had ever written. Zacharias quotes him as saying:

> For several decades we psychologists looked upon the whole matter of sin and moral accountability as a great incubus and acclaimed liberation from it as epoch-making. But at length we have discovered that to be free in this sense, that is to have the excuse of being sick rather than sinful, is to court the danger of also becoming lost. This danger is I believe betokened by the widespread interest in existentialism, which we are presently witnessing. In becoming amoral and ethically neutral and free, we have cut the very roots of our being, lost our deepest sense of selfhood and identity, and with neurotics themselves find ourselves asking who am I, what is my deepest destiny, what does living mean.

These questions were most likely plaguing the mind of one defendant at the Nuremberg trial who said that he was no longer the same person after taking the life of the first innocent man; a sentiment echoed very recently by an American soldier in Michael Moore's *Fahrenheit 9/11*. After the first time, killing becomes easier, getting us back to the slippery slope, which can start with the smallest of transgressions. Fortunately, most of us are not contemplating suicide, and are not in the business of killing people. But don't you sense that every little theft, slight against someone, outburst of abuse, marital indiscretion, gossip or deceit, and jealousy, takes something away from us, making it easier the next time?

I once attended a seminar conducted by one of the world's leading authorities on corporate fraud. He asked us to profile the ideal employee, and predictably the listed attributes included loyalty, trustworthiness, professionalism, etc. He then put alongside our list the attributes of the typical perpetrator of fraud, and they were almost identical: usually a 'good person', who first stole a little, often with the intention to repay it, then a little more, and so on. In an Australian cartoon by Leunig – a person who makes us think more deeply about issues of the day – a boy asks one of those tough questions: 'Father, what is reliability?' The answer goes: 'Reliability is the ability to tell a lie over and over again … to lie and re-lie and re-lie until the lie seems to sound like the truth … that's reliability.'

Beyond the impact of our sin on others and ourselves, have you ever really considered the potential impact on a *holy* God? We could start with his Ten Commandments, which you might note are laws, not guidelines. Significantly, the 'petty misdemeanours' listed above, and where they can lead us, don't stack up too well against the six commandments in the second category. But do you even spare a thought for the four in the first category? The *New Unger's Bible Dictionary* summarises the biblical account of the first four commandments, then the remaining six, in these simple terms:

Our duties to God come first – His being, His worship, His name and His day.

Then come our duties to our fellowmen. They have their beginning in the home. Then they reach out beyond the home circle to all mankind, having regard, first, for our neighbour's life; second, to his wife; third, to his property; fourth, to his position.

Finally, the tenth commandment touches the spring of all moral completeness, the desire of the heart. It is really the intent of the heart that determines the moral character of the act. It cannot be reached by human legislation. It exposes to the conscience the utter failure of an act that might otherwise be blameless.

When God proclaimed these laws, he surely meant them to be abided by *in their totality*, and I don't imagine he intended us to rank them.

In reading the report of an Australian father of two, convicted of manslaughter for brutally killing his wife, I could only ponder how the three players involved – the wife, husband and boyfriend – and the many others affected, might view their own decisions and attitudes in light of the totality of God's law. Plainly each person is a victim of this protracted, heart-breaking saga. The killing followed a history of domestic violence and the breakdown of the couple's marriage. The jury decided on the lesser charge than murder because of 'provocation'. Apparently the wife taunted her husband about her new boyfriend, and is quoted as saying that sex with him repulsed her and 'I'm over you. I should have left you 10 years ago'. After the verdict was announced, her boyfriend echoed the opinion of many, that the legal notion of provocation was outmoded.

As more of our friends and acquaintances experience broken relationships, often after many years of marriage, the tendency is to blame the relationship rather than themselves. But a relationship, comprising separate parts, will not function as long as any individual part is broken. Typically, the newfound love is given precedence over the penetrating questions of 'has wrong been done and to whom, and what must I do to rectify that wrong'. If there is such a thing as right and wrong, there is no option but to address these questions first, and then to strive to rebuild the original relationship, as tough and tedious as that may be. Old fashioned, you might say. Well I take a promise for life to mean just that. And at a practical level, to break a promise means living with destructive unresolved guilt thereafter. Although it takes two to tango, who wants to share their life with someone who has meddled in another's marriage?

Do you think you comprehend the seriousness of sin, as God might see it? Or do you share the following sentiment written by Pamela Bone, a columnist in *The Age*: 'Do people really, in this day and age, want to obey a God who, like a Third World dictator, insists above all on unconditional, absolute reverence to himself (because it must be a him)?'

Surprisingly, despite the fact that most resist God's authority and live a secular life, surveys typically show that the majority say they believe in God. If this is true, there must be profound dissonance at the root of our beings. The nagging voice of our conscience produces restlessness and a sense of insecurity and failure; all in sharp contrast to the peace and joy purportedly intended for us, and instead sadly sought by many through vast quantities of sedatives and stimulants.

Quell the desire for power over others

How much do you yearn for more autonomy to make decisions, either up the ladder at work or in the relationships at home? At a young age I had a taste of power through being the eldest child, class captain, prefect, member on the Student's Representative Council, first student president of my newly founded university college, and president of the national association for my faculty. I was then made a manager in business at a relatively early age.

These leadership positions appealed to my ego and desire for control. However I progressively learned the same lesson as Sir John Harvey-Jones, who devoted his career toward gaining the top job at ICI only to discover, after a few months at the helm, that the levers were not connected to anything. He did not find himself in the position of power that he had imagined. This same realisation influenced my decision to step out of the hierarchy and spend the last sixteen years acting as a 'facilitator', to help liberate the ideas and energy of others.

In the process of clearing the way for us to pursue our own autonomy, under our own power, we construct numerous ways of either rationalising God out of the picture or into a more convenient and less confronting form. In other words, we suppress the truth. As noted earlier, the Bible warns that more than anything else this suppression of truth evokes God's holy anger, leaving him no option but to intervene, or just allow the consequences of our rebellion to flow throughout our lives forever. So the Bible teaches that at the root of our predicament lies the reality of our inability to face the implications of God's holiness and purity.

When talking about post-modernism and scientific modernism, John Milbank, in *Theology and Social Theory beyond Secular Reason*, argues that the exercise of power is at the core of the human condition. Much earlier, Lord Acton, the leading Catholic who argued against making the Pope infallible, famously said that *power tends to corrupt and absolute power corrupts absolutely.*

Like many costly conflicts today, Copernicus' brilliant mathematical calculations – suggesting the sun, not the Earth, is at the centre of the earth – were not part of a genuine theological debate, but rather a historical struggle for power between human institutions. Leaders of the Catholic Church believed that his discoveries offended their biblical interpretation that humankind is at the centre and the sun moves across the sky. They even refused to look down Galileo's telescope, which confirmed Copernicus' theory. But biblical writers did not contradict reality, and neither does our scientific weather report when it announces tomorrow's sunset and sunrise.

Power struggles continue at all levels of church, corporate and family life, often polarised by opposing perceptions of 'what is best'. But when it comes to the crunch of deciding whether to go with the conventional wisdom of the day, or the expert, or a supposed all-knowing, all-wise God, is there any contest, as hard as that can be against the undertow?

Stop justifying ourselves

In the struggle, we constantly try to justify or vindicate our decisions, big and small, with little success. Many of our problems, particularly in relationships, spring from our guilty state. Alain de Botton, disparagingly described by some as a 'populist' philosopher, recently wrote a book about 'status anxiety', with that as its title. He describes it as:

> A worry, so pernicious as to be capable of ruining extended stretches of our lives, that we are in danger of failing to conform to the ideals of success laid down by our society and that we may as a result be stripped of dignity and respect; a worry that we are currently occupying too modest a rung or are about to fall to a lower one.

Someone once said that, in evaluating how well we are going, we spend too much time looking up to the few above, rather than down to the many below. For us in the West that means most of the world. But if there is a God, the ultimate 'measure of our success' must be according to his viewpoint, not that of those around us. As already mentioned, although we fall far short of his standards, guilt and its resultant paralysis can be eradicated through his grace. Christ said to his followers (John 14: 27):

> My peace I give you. I do not give to you as the world gives. Do not let your hearts be troubled and do not be afraid.

We are told that, if we turn back to God and place our faith in Christ instead of other man-made worldviews, we avail ourselves of his unconditional forgiveness, and he will restore our relationship, for eternity. Somehow we are then 'justified' or made perfect *in his sight*, and never need to defend ourselves again. Every day we can awake with the peace of knowing that God perceives us as being holy, through no merit of ours. We are liberated and secure in his acceptance because the 'problem' of his holiness has been dealt with, through *his own crucifixion*.

That is why the cross, if true, is not just a pleasing design for an exquisite piece of jewellery, but the most abhorrent, degrading, despicable and cataclysmic event in all of history, and is at the centre of true Christianity. Such vivid imagery will either evoke indignant outrage or Christ-like humility and courage; two of the most attractive attributes for any person and in sharp contrast to the destructive self-centredness and pride that characterise today's secular world.

But humility and courage to do what?

Translate faith into action

The Bible says: 'As the body without the spirit is dead, so faith without deeds is dead' (James 2: 26). It is interesting to highlight the difference between early Jewish and Greek concepts of faith. The former is about 'active trust', focusing on action and relationships, whereas the latter is more about knowledge and belief. Both perspectives are rightly brought together in the 'faith triangle'. Michael Frost and Alan Hirsch, in their book *The Shaping of Things to Come,* suggest that a 'life of action, movement, energy and striving is the best place for the reflective practices of meditation, prayer, and reflection'.

We have touched on the requirements of God's law as spelt out in his Ten Commandments, the two categories encapsulated succinctly in the OT and quoted by Christ who taught *and showed us* how to live and love:

> Love the Lord your God with all your heart and with all your soul and with all your mind and with all your strength ...
> Love your neighbour as yourself.
>
> ——Matthew 22: 37 & 39

However Christ appears to go even further in his call to radical non-conformity. Take for example what he enunciated in the beatitudes, quoted from the Bible by Gandhi and paraphrased below in compelling terms by Stott.

The first four relate to our humble attitude to God, and the second four to our relationships with others:

Blessed are those who:
- acknowledge their spiritual bankruptcy
- weep over it and our rebellion
- are willing for others to think of them as they see themselves before God
- hunger and thirst for righteousness
- show mercy to those battered by adversity or sin
- are transparently sincere
- seek to play a constructive role in peace making
- patiently bear opposition for the sake of Christ.

According to Stott, these characteristics are in direct collision with those of our world:

Blessed are those who:
- are rich, carefree, brash and well fed
- mind their own business
- are successful even if devious
- are not necessarily pure in heart and are popular.

Christ explains the practical implications of his call to go against the current, *through non-violence alone*. He uses the mercy of God as our standard, by commanding: 'Love your enemies, do good to those who hate you, bless those who curse you, pray for those who mistreat you' (Luke 6: 27-28). Here the implication is that if we return evil for evil we simply add to the evil side of life's ledger, but by returning good for evil we help to re-balance the books.

However he also used a parable about a business manager to underline the need for his followers to be no less *shrewd* than those of 'this world', as evidenced through their resourcefulness. In describing how we should resist evil, Wink shows how Christ illustrated the difference between submissive passivity and creative, assertive non-violence. He used three well-known examples: 'If someone strikes you on the right cheek, turn to him the other also. And if someone wants to sue you and take your tunic, let him have your cloak as well. If someone forces you to go one mile, go with him two miles' (Matthew 5: 39-41).

By the by, this is a classic case of needing to understand the context of biblical passages to avoid missing their full significance. Christ was talking to the poor and oppressed in the days of 'honour and shaming'. His audience knew that to be struck on the right cheek required being humiliatingly slapped with the back of the right hand, rather than punched with the left, because it was socially unacceptable to raise the hand reserved for unclean tasks. By turning the left cheek, they could only be punched by the right hand, not backhanded (try it for yourself); but only equals fought with fists. So the inferior was no longer cowed. Of course he could expect a beating, but if the people adopted this tactic *en masse* the superior would eventually fuel a social revolution.

Similarly, the audience had been stripped of all their land and possessions due to exorbitant interest rates and taxes, and frequently were sent to court, unable to pay their bills. It was even legal to take the debtor's outer cloak as collateral, although it had to be returned each evening. According to Wink, to suggest the debtor strip naked in the courtroom by removing his undergarments as well would shame the creditor and 'register a stunning protest against the system that created his debt'.

Christ's third example refers to the Roman code that only allowed forced labour to carry a soldier's pack for one mile, and there were penalties for contravening this code. Imagine then a soldier pleading with an insistent slave that he hand his pack back, his feeling of superiority quashed.

These illustrations suggest that major change can have small beginnings, and that coercion is permissible as long as there is no violence. I am reminded of how one person on a motor bike with a couple of dogs can so effectively, yet quietly, cajole a large mob of sheep to move without fuss in the desired direction. The illustrations also throw out the challenge to adopt creative non-violent resistance tactics in today's culture. Interestingly, African women stripped naked in front of bulldozers driven by puritanical Afrikaners to play their part in the overthrow of apartheid!

Insist that justice be done

There are still two practical questions in relation to the issue of justice – what is humanity's role in deciding its scope and administering it? The Bible says that the ultimate lawgiver allows for the appointment of governments to legislate *human* law to protect people and their property, and policing and judiciary authorities to administer it. It also warns that the power vested in all institutions, corporations, churches, families and other organisations, comes from God, hence they are ultimately accountable to him for their vocation – the wellbeing of those they serve. Although flawed, we have to rely on numerous corporate bodies whilst we attempt to engender change.

For example, we look to legal institutions to be more objective in their treatment of the wrongdoer than those who have been hurt. Many would say the pendulum has now swung too far at the expense of the victim, but only yesterday there were two instances that reinforced in my mind the need for independent adjudication. I was extremely angry to discover that an intruder had broken into our house, and fortunately for both of us, we did not meet on the stairs. This happened to follow my reading of a passage in the Koran, because my daughter is working in Afghanistan. I learnt that a husband should beat his wife for disobedience to him, but only after giving her two chances to change her attitude – by first admonishing her and then not sharing her bed (Sūrah 4: 34).

How quick and self-righteous we can be about our moral judgement of others. Yet according to the Bible, God alone judges how we stand in relation to his moral law, and we are warned about the danger of hypocrisy:

 Do not judge, or you too will be judged. For in the same way you judge others, you will be judged, and with the measure you use, it will be measured to you.

——Matthew 7: 1

Why do you look at the speck of sawdust in your brother's eye and pay no attention to the plank in your own eye? How can you say to your brother, 'Let me take the speck out of your eye,' when all the time there is a plank in your own eye? You hypocrite, first take the plank out of your own eye, and then you will see clearly to remove the speck from your brother's eye.

——Matthew 7: 3-5

This ancient teaching is actually about what modern psychologists call 'projection'. A useful test we can all apply to ourselves is the question 'what do I least like in that other person?'.

Frequently the answers are actually those things we like least in ourselves, which is an acute reminder that we are as flawed as our enemies. When the crowd accused a woman of adultery, the punishment of the day being stoning to death, Christ said: 'If any one of you is without sin, let him be the first to throw a stone at her' (John 8: 7).

Because this story seems to conflict sharply with the appalling punishments an angry God allegedly meted out to many in the OT, many conclude that he is cruel and heartless, and certainly not worthy of their allegiance. Wink and Sproul cast different light on this issue. Wink suggests that 'God was working through violence to expose violence for what it is and to reveal the divine nature as non-violent'. The ultimate triumph was Christ's death on the cross; something 'the powers that be' would not have done had they realised they were exposing the horror and futility of violence.

Sproul concludes that God is incredibly merciful to allow *any* to survive, because we have all broken his law, and he made it clear from the outset that the penalty must be death. It is also sobering to remember that the loving God of the NT is the same God. The bedfellow of love *must* be justice; we cannot have, *and actually do not want*, one without the other. If this is all true, here is the recurring problem: we are in trouble and seem unable to help ourselves.

The Bible explains, to a world where the individual demands his or her 'rights' and 'freedom', that we have actually become captive to our own selfish desires by eschewing *God's right as our maker*; the pot has spurned the potter. We are like the astronaut, who appears to have absolute freedom to move in space, but can only twist and turn around his or her centre of gravity.

How many times do you think and say 'I have lost control'? How many senior managers, and parents, have discovered that to regain control they must first learn how to relinquish it, and then live in hope? Consequently, the word 'empowerment' has become the panacea for many 'change agents' in business, but managers cannot directly empower subordinates any more than parents can empower their children. The best they can do is create an environment where their charges are free to empower themselves, *if they so desire and are able*.

Rely on a greater power to resume control

We all know that freedom without rules leads to anarchy. For all the change agents out there, Christ offered what might be the ultimate 'transformation process', that starts with freeing us from the dominance of ego, *so that we are enabled to be and do what God intended*. We can then read the Ten Commandments as promises rather than prohibitions – Christ promises, for those who submit their all, that the *Holy Spirit* or *Counsellor* can and will empower us. He will provide the strength, guidance and reassurance required to develop a holy character, one of integrity or wholeness. Because we are so deeply entrenched in the ways of the world, the Bible warns that 'dying to self', as symbolised on the cross, will be a gradual, life-long battle of being transformed into the likeness of Christ.

The Bible lists examples of the 'fruits of the Spirit' as being love, joy, peace, patience, kindness, goodness, faithfulness, gentleness and self-control. Can you imagine a business running along these lines? Can you imagine coming home to a place that feels like that?

However, there is one important distinction for those whose main pursuit is happiness: we are promised fundamental changes to our character but not to our *personality*. For example, Stott says that extroverts and introverts will continue as before, but the former will be easier to live with, and the latter will find it easier to live with themselves! In *Journey of Personality, August 2003*, a team led by Avshalom Caspi of London's Institute of Psychiatry, reported on a trial that started in 1980 with 1,000 three-year-olds.

When re-assessed at 26, these people showed little difference in the main personality traits they exhibited as toddlers.

From my experience, we not only yearn for an ultimate reference point, or set of co-ordinates against which to navigate our journey, but also for role models, and some wise facilitation along the way. The Bible presents us with the extraordinary notion of the *triune* nature of God: one in three and three in one. Alister McGrath, who started out as a biochemist and is now a reputed theologian at Oxford University, wrote in his book *Understanding the Trinity*:

> No one picture, image or model of God is good enough ... The first model is that of a transcendent God who lies beyond the world as its source and creator; the second is the human face of God, revealed in the person of Jesus Christ; the third is that of the immanent God who is present and active throughout his creation.

This is why people in church often say 'the grace', a blessing quoted directly from the Bible: 'May the grace of the Lord Jesus Christ, and the love of God, and the fellowship of the Holy Spirit be with you all' (2 Corinthians 13: 14).

Such a mystery, which by definition is beyond our ability to comprehend fully, elucidate through analogy, or explain through human language, raises the most ancient questions that divide humanity: is there such a thing as truth, and if so, is it only as I want to see it?

The *Oxford Dictionary* defines truth in these terms: 'Being in accordance with fact or actuality, reason or correct principles or accepted standard, rightly so-called, genuine, not spurious or hybrid or counterfeit or merely apparent.' This definition is another expression of the rationality and reality tests, and requires us to be prudent in any assertions we might make. Harry

Frankfurt, Professor Emeritus of Philosophy at Princeton University, has written a serious analysis of a subject we are all very familiar with, entitled *On Bullshit*. Here is a short extract from the book:

> Someone who ceases to believe in the possibility of identifying certain statements as true and others as false can have only two alternatives. The first is to desist both from efforts to tell the truth and from efforts to deceive. This would mean refraining from making any assertion whatever about the facts. The second alternative is to continue making assertions that purport to describe the way things are, but that cannot be anything except bullshit.

We can look at things through rose tinted glasses or a jaundiced eye – friends see us in one way and enemies another; the artist teaches not to over-paint or over-write, because the human eye fills in the gaps. Only a transcendent God could have a comprehensive, perfect perception of reality, and determine if, how much, when and through what means, revelation of that perception will take place. Hopefully, he would also deal with the fallibility of our senses, by guiding us as we ponder such things and progressively learn how we were originally meant to live in harmony; internally, with each other, and with him.

We have been promised that through *prayer* we can discern the will of the Creator and Sustainer, thus enabling us to synchronise our wills, rather than work at cross-purposes. Yet it is an extremely difficult discipline, because of our weariness through struggle, and it being the place where we engage in the spiritual battle between good and evil, not simply add emails to a massive inbox in the sky. Polkinghorne uses the neat metaphor of a laser beam to portray the power of prayer and partnership with God. Physicists describe laser light as being 'coherent', because the crests and troughs of the waves are all in step, thus avoiding the cancellation of each other.

None of us are ever 'good enough' to pray; yet we are told God always graciously hears and answers prayer. Of course we might expect that if we ask him for something that from his perspective is not good in itself, or good for us, his answer will be no, like that of any caring parent. Someone once said: 'If it were the case that whatever we ask God was pledged to give, I for one would never pray again.' Then there is the issue of God's apparent delayed response, perhaps because the request is not timely, or the wider spiritual battle is causing the hold up. We either conclude that God is impotent, or accept that we cannot comprehend this deep mystery and aggressively continue to pray that justice will eventually prevail.

Strangely, Christ taught us to pray to our *Father*, as totally dependent *children*, simply, without hypocrisy and vain empty repetition; thus the Lord's Prayer. The British theologian J I Packer says that what distinguishes a Christian is someone who has God as his or her Father. The Jews would never dream of using such an intimate term for the holy God. Muslims have 99 titles for God, but not one is Father. Incidentally, love does not feature in the 99 either. If God is our heavenly Father, it makes eminent sense to me as an earthly father that he will provide the eyes and ears of those who wish to see and hear, all they need to know about the truth; through all the media at his disposal – the world around us, history, our inner selves and the written word.

Through the prophet Isaiah, God said: 'For my thoughts are not your thoughts, neither are your ways my ways … As the heavens are higher than the earth, so are my ways higher than your ways and my thoughts than your thoughts' (Isaiah 55: 8-9). But also according to the Bible, those who turn back to God are given 'the mind of Christ' by his Spirit – the only way we can begin to glimpse the mind of God.

Hence Christ commanded us to *read the scriptures*. Like prayer, this is another discipline that requires perseverance. Incidentally, discipline and perseverance are strong themes throughout the Bible (as opposed to some modern experts' views on disciplining children). In watching the stoic reaction by the locals to the London bombings, it was tempting to think that these are particularly British traits! Here are just two places in the Bible where perseverance is mentioned:

> … we know that suffering produces perseverance; perseverance, character; and character, hope.
>
> ——Romans 5: 3-4

> … make every effort to add to your faith goodness; and to goodness, knowledge; and to knowledge, self-control; and to self-control, perseverance; and to perseverance, godliness; and to godliness, brotherly kindness; and to brotherly kindness, love.
>
> ——2 Peter 1: 5-7

Stott says that if the Bible is the living word of God, it can neither be read like a newspaper, novel or textbook, nor in a hostile manner. God's Spirit will only illuminate our understanding when we approach it with an open, humble, prayerful, reverent and expectant mind; thinking, pondering, meditating, discussing and debating. William Tyndale, the great master of language whose influence has been likened to that of Shakespeare, said 'the plough boy could grasp it better than the Pope'. By the by, as a result of spending his life translating and distributing the Bible's first English translation to the ordinary person, which in the process took literacy a quantum leap forward, Tyndale was condemned as a heretic in 1536, strangled, and burned for his trouble.

But beware, says biblical scholar Stott; this simplicity applies to the fundamentals of salvation and ethics of discipleship; many other things are much harder to understand. Therefore we need to complement our individual study by exploring with fellow travellers, further reading, and listening to qualified teachers or expositors. What is more, Stott counsels the grassroots and scholars to listen to and learn from each other in order to avoid individualism and elitism. He also advises that, in view of today's hugely complex ethical issues, followers of Christ must speak from the word of God authoritatively *and* tentatively, the ultimate test of authenticity being their practical submission to it in their daily lives.

Where there are apparent discrepancies, Stott says we should not prematurely accuse or manipulate, but rather seek to 'synthesise and harmonise', to maintain a balance that respects the intention of the biblical writer. We should allow the scripture to explain itself. When we cannot resolve apparent discrepancies, he says that it is *more Christian* to confess our ignorance than arrogantly claim the Bible to be flawed. He asks where we would be without the Bible – 'a lamp to our feet and a light to our path', an impregnable rock on which to stand in heavy seas, a guide, compass, map' – and concludes that our main attitude should be one of extreme gratitude.

So it seems that followers of Christ need to pray and read for discernment. We are also told that such activities will liberate our inbuilt desire to worship God and celebrate the blessings of life with deep thankfulness. Many biblical characters were ecstatic in their praise, and according to the Bible Christ himself was not averse to enjoying a good party.

Celebrate life and overcome the fear of death

Worship is another word we use selectively, but why just expend it on the transient celebrities and sports stars of our day, when it might be the greatest expression of which we are capable?

Archbishop William Temple once said: 'Worship is the submission of all of my nature to God, it is the quickening of conscience by His holiness, nourishment of mind by His truth, purifying of imagination by His beauty, opening of the heart to His love, and submission of will to His purpose.'

Much of this book is about rationality, which raises the possibility of worshipping God with our *minds*. But it is also about reality, and many vouch for the sheer joy of focusing their *hearts* on his greatness, generosity and love, and contemplating the suffering he bears alongside them in their pain. They accept that God does not promise to remove all pain, but is always faithful in being with them in their troubles. They would say there are numerous opportunities for such a deep emotional experience, from weeping at the bedside of the dying, to holding your newborn child, admiring a stunning sunset, or being part of a congregation united in song and hushed silent reflection about the generous life and death of Christ, who took the sting out of death.

How much does the reality of death influence your decision-making? Woody Allen famously said: 'I wouldn't mind dying so much if it wasn't that I would be dead at the end of it.' It is human to fear the process of dying, but another thing entirely to contemplate death. Especially if we heed the repeated warning of God's many messengers that eventually all will be subjected to the perfect justice we deserve. Although this is very reassuring when we think about the despots who have escaped punishment in this world, Christ made plain that every one of us will have to give a final account, adjudged by a loving and holy creator. And he said: 'What good will it be for a man if he gains the whole world yet forfeits his soul?' (Matthew 16: 26).

Alexander Solzhenitsyn suffered torture and deprivation in the Russian Gulag. As Wink would say, he drew the sting of evil in his own body, knowing his captors could easily take his life, but believing that none could touch his soul.

However for the pragmatist, there is no final account. The agnostic says 'I don't know if God exists or not', and then proceeds to denigrate the idea of God. The existentialist anti-hero approaches all he has to look forward to – the here and now – with courage and gusto, 'because life is meaningless I am going to create my own destiny my way. I am going to laugh in the face of fate'. In reading the biblical words attributed to God, 'Before me every knee will bow', do you think that these people are extraordinarily brave, or extraordinarily foolish? Zacharias says in *The Real Face of Atheism*:

> The atheist risks everything for the present and the future, on the basis of a belief that we are uncaused by any intelligent being. We just happen to be here. That one is willing to live and die in that belief is a very high price to pay for conjecture.

I once listened to someone praising the bravery of Todd Beamer on September 11 in front of a friend of mine, a successful and thoughtful CEO of a major global corporation. Via his cell phone, Beamer – a Christian – was heard to say 'let's roll' as he led the charge to overpower the terrorists flying Flight 93 to Washington DC on that fateful day. When I ventured that my friend would have been equally brave he modestly concurred. But when further prompted, he unflinchingly commented that, on impact with the ground, *his* lights would have simply gone out.

Death need not hold any fear if it means we just fall asleep and enter oblivion forever, but we should at least pause to compare this view with Beamer's conviction that he would be reunited with his wife and kids in heaven; or with Christ's shocking portrayal of life in hell. This is the fundamental point of divergence for secularism, other popular schools of thought, and the picture so graphically painted by Christ, with massive implications for the way we live before we die.

Secularists either say there is no eternal, or if there is, we can know nothing about it. Hence many resort to worrying about accumulating material wealth, so that 'we can eat drink and be merry, for tomorrow we die'. On the other hand, although God allegedly created all good things for us to enjoy to the full, and Christ exhorted us not to worry, he also said 'store up for yourselves treasures in heaven' (Matthew 6: 20). He teaches that we are created for eternity, and that there are abiding absolutes against which life can be evaluated on this planet and beyond, rather than the shifting riptides of here and now. Clearly there can be no viable hybrid of these contradictory positions.

At your stage in life you may be thinking that it is premature to be even contemplating death and eternity. In my thirties a lifetime seemed a very long time too. But in my sixties it has shrunk to a brief moment on the stage of history, and the notion of eternity has become inescapable. I certainly relate to this poignant quote from the Bible: 'As for man, his days are like grass, he flourishes like a flower of the field; the wind blows over it and it is gone, and its place remembers it no more' (Psalm 103: 15-16).

CHAPTER EIGHT

OTHER COURSES

MAKING RADICAL OR INCREMENTAL CHANGE AND
REAFFIRMING THE STATUS QUO

In this hugely complex area I have only endeavoured to highlight three alternative courses that might be taken. These are: 1) to adopt some form of New Age spirituality, 2) to change the church, or 3) to stay with the evolving conventional wisdom.

Adopt New Age spirituality

MacLaine says that perhaps self-realisation is what Moses, Christ, Buddha, Pythagoras, Plato and all the religious and philosophical sages down through the ages have been trying to tell us – 'know yourself and the truth will set you free'. We are rescued from within, not from without.

Like MacLaine, many see our time as the harbinger of a new age, moving out of the yang (masculine) age of Pisces (doubt, disillusionment and confusion), which began before Christ, into the yin (feminine) age of Aquarius (faith, enlightenment and clarity), which some think began in the 1960s with the counterculture, and others believe has not yet fully arrived. Although there are people who dismiss these ideas as naïve and harmless aberrations, they deserve close examination because they have entered our culture through the media, science fiction, schools, universities and influential business courses. It is estimated that there are over ten million followers of various New Age groups worldwide.

How much do you know about this phenomenon? Definitions of the New Age Movement abound, which in fact is a misnomer because there is no organisation *per se*; it represents a loose collection of many diverse constituencies. In *A Dictionary of New Age Terminology* (see www.eastrovedica.com/html/newagedictionary.htm), examples include: environmentalists, nuclear-freeze proponents, Marxist-socialist theoreticians, clairvoyants, spiritually evolved Masters, gemologists, parapsychologists, sufis, yogis, shamans, theosophists, peace activists, alternative energy people, holistic and psychic healers, human potentialists; and there are many more. The common link is described as 'people advanced in consciousness and committed to Universal Love'.

Stott says the similarly random collection of New Age ideas appears to have twelve strands:

- evolutionary optimism – our potential for transformation
- Eastern pantheistic mysticism – you are God and God is you
- human potential movement – you can create your own reality
- astrology – predicting the future through horoscopes
- spiritism – trance channelling of spirit guides
- occult practices – paranormal experiences
- reincarnation – karma and cosmic justice
- science fiction – UFOs and extra-terrestrials
- green movement – peace, justice and the integrity of creation
- alternative medicine – acupuncture, biofeedback
- subatomic physics and Heisenberg's Uncertainty Principle
- Western materialism

In my search for more information to compare New Age thinking with Christ's teaching, I came across these quotes in Webster's New Age Encyclopaedia:

New Agers claim no single external source of authority – but their primary scriptures are the Bible, the Bhagavad Gita and A Course in Miracles. All scripture is subject to the authority of 'the god within'.

A major idea in New Age thinking is that of the 'Christ Consciousness'. They teach that Christ is the 'only begotten son of God' from the beginning and that Jesus, at best, merely expressed the Christ. This idea of 'Christ Consciousness' asserts that Jesus was not the only person to achieve 'Christ Consciousness', but so also did Buddha, Krishna, and Mohammed. Many New Agers also like to say that Jesus spent 18 years in India absorbing Hinduism and the teachings of Buddha. New Agers believe that Jesus received the 'Christ Consciousness' at his baptism.

New Agers find nothing which is of the nature of sin. They speak of 'troublesome desires' which appear to be misdirected natural human impulses which are hardly sinful. Since New Agers believe that each person is part of god, thereby having endless potential for self-improvement, sin (as defined by the Jesus cult) does not exist. They think that any perceived lack that man might have is merely a lack of enlightenment. Generally, they teach that the idea of Jesus, or anyone else, having to die for our sins is a gross corruption of truth.

The Jesus cult view of Lucifer or Satan as the head of a tightly organised system of 'evil' is seldom held by New Agers. Rather, Lucifer is often described in Biblical terms as a being of light.

While many New Agers eschew the material world as an illusion, many others attach great importance to artefacts, relics, and sacred objects: Tibetan bells, pyramids, crystals, and a plethora of electronic energy devices. Crystals are the favourite New Age object. These are not only thought to have healing powers, but are considered programmable, like a computer, if one just concentrates hard enough. Other

New Age symbols would include the rainbow; butterfly; pyramid; eye in triangle; unicorn; swastika; yin-yang; pentagram; concentric circles; rays of light; crescent moon; etc. Most of these symbols are derived from Christian or other religious sources.

MacLaine, in talking about her experience in the Peruvian Andes, says in her book *Out On A Limb*:

> I tried to piece it all together, the continual connections of God and spirit, and love and karma, and other worlds and cosmic justice and basic kindness and spiritual enlightenment, and Jesus and flying machines, and the golden rule and advanced civilisation, and gods who came in chariots of fire, etc. Was it all beginning to make sense? Perhaps humans were part of an overall cosmic plan that had been in effect for thousands and thousands of years.

The appeal is this genuine quest for harmony, an integral or holistic worldview; but the result is confusion, an uneasy blend of Eastern mysticism and Western materialism, science and superstition, yin and yang, feminine and masculine, space and time, physics and metaphysics, ancient wisdom and new consciousness. Stott says there appear to be three underlying beliefs or affirmations: all is one (monism), all is God (pantheism), and all is well (evolutionism); all seemingly uneasy bedfellows.

Monism leads adherents to the view that the ultimate status of consciousness is when all boundaries and all dualisms have been transcended, and all individuality dissolves into a universal, undifferentiated 'oneness'.

Pantheism, where all things, animate or inanimate, are part of a single, impersonal divine energy, leads people to believe that *everyone is God*. MacLaine says this is the one basic spiritual law that would make the world a happier and healthier place.

Hence the fundamental human predicament is ignorance of one's true identity, not sin and guilt. In other words, it is metaphysical rather than moral; the alienation humans experience is not alienation from God, but alienation from our true selves. Therefore we need enlightenment, gnosis (knowledge of spiritual mysteries), not forgiveness. This higher or altered consciousness comes, not through drugs, but through techniques like yoga, transcendental meditation, Werner Erhard's EST, visualisation, crystals or meditation on the chakras (according to Hinduism the life energy nodes in the body, placed on an intermediate layer which lies between the spirit and the earthly body to manage different aspects of earthly life).

Evolutionism, as we saw earlier, is about being profoundly optimistic; because we are 'gods' we have unlimited potential for transformation; through higher consciousness we can bring an era of peace, harmony and happiness – individual, social and planetary transformation.

MacLaine says:

Imitate Christ, because Christ worked out his soul's progression to near perfection and others can do what he did. Know your potential, that's what it takes. Every individual is the creator and controller of his own destiny. Each individual is a co-creator with God. The process will probably include several reincarnations, and our personal transformation will lead to the transformation of society and of the planet until there is one culture and one religion embracing us all.

I expect you can already see that the central tenets of MacLaine's belief system simply cannot be reconciled with the teaching of Christ, who clearly distinguished between two times – 'this age' and 'the age to come, eternal life' (Luke 18: 30).

Change the church

Many identify fatal flaws in 'me-centric' New Age thinking and secularism, and limitations in other belief systems, so try to drag the out-of-touch Western church into the twenty-first century. Most conspicuous are those making the local church an integral part of the community and those striving to relate to contemporary culture. Well-meaning people have either revamped the way they project themselves, their style, the message, or all three. But the results are mixed, due to the many risks and inherent hazards of initiating change.

These risks are particularly acute in creative attempts to rearticulate 'brand values' in business. When sales slow or markets change, huge marketing research, consultancy, advertising and internal communications budgets are often allocated to 're-position the brand' and launch new communications programmes. Modern churches have borrowed some of these marketing techniques, including reliance on charismatic leaders and celebrities to 'embellish the brand', and slick multi-media productions. Frequently, however, commercial attempts at re-branding, which may even involve changing the brand name altogether, fail because there is no real improvement in the product or service, or because the perceived negative connotations of the old brand are so overwhelming.

So what is the 'product' in this case? What do we actually mean by the word 'church'? Typically we think of it as the charming old building down the road, or an organisation, or an assortment of organisations, or even a hierarchy. In contrast, the Bible describes it as 'the body of Christ', comprising those who have put their faith in Christ as their means for eternal reconciliation with God, and who strive to live by God's law. According to Stott's reading of the Bible, Christ's vision for his church requires four elements to be kept in balance – faithful adherence to the truth, holiness, mission, and unity. Logically therefore, man-made organisations that do not meet the above criteria are on shaky ground when they call themselves churches.

Today's churches present a nightmare for the brand consultant, because of the heavy baggage associated with the terms Church, Christian and Christianity, and the ongoing emergence of new flavours. Divisions are not new to the 'established church', one of our most ancient institutions. The Orthodox and Catholic Churches both lay claim to being 'the original one and only'. Centuries ago the Protestants broke away from the Catholics, and they are now broken up into denominations like the Anglicans, Baptists, Methodists, Presbyterians, Lutherans, etc. There are even distinct camps within each denomination, typified by the Anglicans who range from 'high church' Anglo-Catholics to the 'low church', representing a spectrum from the legalistic, ritualistic and ceremonial, to the informal. Essentially the problem becomes one of distinguishing between presentational style and theological content, and what is core and peripheral within the latter.

Currently we have a high profile clash between the 'evangelicals' and 'liberals', a division that cuts across denominations. There are even differing hues of evangelicalism, namely the 'conservatives' and 'charismatics' – particularly the 'Pentecostal movement'. Evangelical groups have in common a belief in the Bible and a personal relationship with God, and a desire to proclaim salvation through Christ, but differ noticeably in style and theological *emphasis*. In their differing quests to 'modernise' Christianity, evangelicals are described by liberals as 'theologically conservative'. The Pentecostals counter by saying they have modernised their *style* to appeal to young people yet remained faithful to the *biblical message*, as opposed to the liberals who have done the reverse.

The word 'evangelism' evokes a hostile reaction in our 'tolerant' pluralistic world. The sceptical media uses derisive and divisive tags to distinguish between the so-called rigid, authoritarian, bible-bashing conservatives, the more moderate, socially open and progressive conservatives, and the weird charismatics infatuated with the Holy Spirit. Conservative evangelicals are written off as dry and heartless fundamentalists, and the Pentecostal movement as a syrupy cocktail of pop, conservative morality, and blind biblical adherence. Another group cops plenty of stick as well – the growing body of high profile preachers of the 'prosperity gospel', who are slotted in the same category as motivational gurus expounding on how to succeed and get rich.

By adopting the (fading) charismatic business leadership model, and attempting primarily to capture people's emotions, the church can fall for the alluring 'heart before head' tack of secular existentialism that bombards us from the billboard and television screen. Consequently, some see a distinctive brand of 'religion' being projected to impressionable young people, in packed big auditoriums on big screens backed by big sound, as the hip alternative to the hip culture of the day, rather than what might be the enduring Truth worthy of very serious consideration. Others say the Bible makes it clear that our intrinsic desire to worship should not just be expressed in exhilarating group activity, but as an embedded attitude that permeates all we think and do.

Older people in the church and the wider world do our youth a great disservice by lamenting their apparent superficiality without attempting to exercise their minds. I wonder at what age this 'superficiality' sets in, as I doubt that little children are now any different than mine were – from the age of three they started to ask the 'what and why' questions. Research indicates a trend away from the stereotypical image of over-stimulated youth, suffering Attention Deficit/Hyperactivity Disorder and thriving on hyper-reality. So is the only solution to replace well-constructed and challenging sermons with the dreaded PowerPoint and more 'entertaining' interactive methods?

Obviously greater emphasis could also be placed on helping the embattled local clergy to lift their game, both in delivery and content, and perhaps most importantly to *embody* the message. (Bearing in mind this should not just apply to the clergy.)

At a different level, and at the risk of continuing to sound like a grumpy old man, I am also inclined to question the importance some attach to informality when relating to the young. Enrolments at expensive private schools continue to go up, partly because parents *and* children appreciate the need for order and discipline. This is occurring despite steep rises in fees and the view by some experts that constraints are the enemy of creativity and empowerment. The casual dressing fad in the office was introduced to promote creativity and informality, yet increased sloppiness in thought and application has prompted some companies to swing back the pendulum; often to the relief of the older staff challenged by their wardrobe.

Are some evangelicals trying too hard to be cool, even at the expense of the message? Media guru Marshall McLuhan, a master of aphorisms as shown in the title of his book, *The Medium is the Massage*, makes the point that the message is greatly influenced by the delivery system. At the risk of oversimplifying the theological differences between evangelicals, it seems that part of the problem is the varying emphasis given to God the Father, God the Son, and God the Holy Spirit.

The idea of God being 'one in essence and three in person' is central to Christ's teaching; interestingly, the Bible's opening sentence uses a plural form for God's name. Rather than being divisive, the Trinity can be viewed as the ultimate expression of *unity in diversity*, of course an incomprehensible mystery, confused by many, and conveniently despatched as yet another myth or absurdity by others, particularly the liberal wing of the church. The Trinity also provides a definitive model for the Bible's metaphor of the inherent unity and diversity of the genuine church: 'Now the body is not made up of one part but of many' (1 Corinthians 12: 14).

The greatest peril for those evangelicals deploying techniques used in the secular worlds of marketing and politics is to allow the re-invention of their style to soften and distort the message. This is the very accusation levelled at the liberals, who seem driven by the desire to make the message more 'acceptable', and in the process also risk getting caught in a rip of their making. Stott likens such customisation to the gardener strolling along his flower patch picking the blooms of his choosing. As a young man disillusioned with the church, I too attempted to customise the story to suit my predilections, and a long time elapsed before I could accept that it all centres on what the purportedly unchanging and enduring Christ of the Bible taught and lived.

Liberals are led by people who do not subscribe to the dominance of the experiential, and who do not retreat from reason to a fortress of blind faith. They appear to focus their energies on aggressively attacking many fundamental tenets of the established church. The Rt Rev John Shelby Spong, retired bishop of Newark, prolific writer and 1999 Humanist of the Year, illustrates this in *A Call for a New Reformation*. He sets the scene by asserting that science and psychology have rendered the biblical account and mainline churches out of step with modern times. He says: 'This Reformation will recognise that the *pre-modern* concepts in which Christianity has traditionally been carried will never again speak to the *post-modern* world we now inhabit.' He calls the Christians of the world to realise the following:

1. Theism, as a way of defining God, is dead. So most theological God-talk is today meaningless. A new way to speak of God must be found.
2. Since God can no longer be conceived in theistic terms, it becomes nonsensical to seek to understand Jesus as the

incarnation of the theistic deity. So the Christology of the ages is bankrupt.

3. The biblical story of the perfect and finished creation from which human beings fell into sin is pre-Darwinian mythology and post-Darwinian nonsense.

4. The virgin birth, understood as literal biology, makes Christ's divinity, as traditionally understood, impossible.

5. The miracle stories of the New Testament can no longer be interpreted in a post-Newtonian world as supernatural events performed by an incarnate deity.

6. The view of the cross as the sacrifice for the sins of the world is a barbarian idea based on primitive concepts of God and must be dismissed.

7. Resurrection is an action of God. Jesus was raised into the meaning of God. It therefore cannot be a physical resuscitation occurring inside human history.

8. The story of the Ascension assumed a three-tiered universe and is therefore not capable of being translated into the concepts of a post-Copernican space age.

9. There is no external, objective, revealed standard writ in scripture or on tablets of stone that will govern our ethical behaviour for all time.

10. Prayer cannot be a request made to a theistic deity to act in human history in a particular way.

11. The hope for life after death must be separated forever from the behaviour control mentality of reward and punishment. The Church must abandon, therefore, its reliance on guilt as a motivator of behaviour.

12. All human beings bear God's image and must be respected for what each person is. Therefore, no external description of one's being, whether based on race, ethnicity, gender or sexual orientation, can properly be used as the basis for either rejection or discrimination.

Here is the problem for the man or woman in the street seeking practical answers. First, he or she sees the church caught up in an internal struggle, made topical by the apparent thrust for political power by the evangelicals, within and beyond the church, and the backlash of other factions, who some would say have been out-manoeuvred at their own game of behind-the-scenes wrangling. One example is the story behind the recent struggles within the Anglican Diocese of Sydney, as reported by Chris McGillion in his book *The Chosen Ones*. Perhaps leaders from all sides should be mindful of the inherent risks of such power, amply demonstrated through history by other institutions claiming to be God's only true church, and Christ's strikingly different example.

Secondly, he or she hears numerous theologians, of apparently equal scholarship, say that people like Spong (and the like-minded scholars of the Jesus Seminar) may have started with the worthy intent to make the message relevant to today, but have gone much too far, and are preoccupied with vilifying the established church and its Christianity. Many criticisms by liberals over the centuries are obviously justified, although they would show more balance by affirming countless enduring gifts to the world as well. Their focus on the negative more than positive is the very argument they level against the church.

When addressing what God is like, what Jesus actually said and did, and the reliability of the Bible, liberal scholars risk imposing their preferences without allowing for the possibility of a *transcendent* Creator having a different and an infinitely bigger picture. Are they repeating history by putting their authority above the Bible, through elevating their 'scholarly analyses' above those recorded by biblical eyewitnesses and historians of the calibre of Luke? Are they merely creating yet another religion of human design, that is even tinged with secularist hues? Is Spong's proposed alternative simply another attempt to understand the 'here and now', based on his interpretation of science, knowledge of psychology, and use of selected and often literally 're-translated' biblical texts?

Sproul says that, in their rush to show that they understand what our world means by tolerance, many in the church have by default embraced pluralism, which by definition must allow contradictory views of God.

Different camps accuse each other of making specific assertions and logical inferences that don't stand up, but such accusations often only lead to inconclusive, tit for tat, endless debate. There will always be many difficult questions to consider. Alternatively, if you want to stick with changing the church and not bail out, you can get back in the helicopter, look again at the terrain we have covered, and consider which line of reasoning makes more sense, however unpalatable: the overall thrust of the Bible's account of creation, humanity's rebellion, and God's solution in Christ, or Spong's New Reformation.

The interested observer will conclude that the Bible's account of God's character and his involvement in the affairs of humanity (including OT carnage), is either true or not. Christ was either Mary's son and God's son, one personality and two natures, fully God and fully human, or not. The alleged miracles of the virgin birth and the resurrection were the beginning and the end of Christ's existence on earth, or not. The liberals are either strikingly right, or shockingly wrong.

Liberals seem to place great store on intellectual respectability, and some perhaps need to be reminded that this can only be earned through rigour, balance and humility in argument. Stott, who exhibits these traits in abundance, surmises that many may find it very difficult to face the ridicule of being seen as naïve and credulous enough to believe in miracles. In vivid contrast, he uses as an example the humility and courage of Mary. She readily accepted the cost of participating in the fulfilment of God's purpose – the enormous stigma of bearing an illegitimate child in her day.

Considering the above, how would you rate the efforts of those who strive to invent and promote a more coherent and compelling scenario than that offered by the Christ of the Bible? The Bible is unequivocal when it says: 'See to it that no one takes you captive through hollow and deceptive philosophy, which depends on human tradition and the basic principles of this world rather than on Christ' (Colossians 2: 8).

Chesterton scoffs in scathing terms at apparently vain attempts of human beings to create their own view of the world:

> So you are the Creator and Redeemer of the world: but what a small world it must be! What a little heaven you must inhabit, with angels no bigger than butterflies! How sad it must be to be God; and an inadequate God! Is there really no life fuller and no love more marvellous than yours; and is it really in your small and painful pity that all flesh must put its faith? How much happier you would be, how much more of you there would be, if the hammer of a higher God could smash your small cosmos, scattering the stars like spangles, and leave you in the open, free like other men to look up as well as down!

In conclusion, coming down once again to our tiny speck in the cosmos, I suspect a professional brand consultant would reassuringly point out that it's not only the church that's suffering a crisis of confidence, but also many big brands – one survey has shown that 40 of the top 75 world brands are losing value. Today's consumers are increasingly savvy; they say they want the real thing in local markets, not brands in supermarkets, and real people to deal with, not pre-programmed digitised voices. The emerging 'iPod generation', successor to Generation X, is even into 'ethical chic', preferring brands that contribute profits to causes. Most importantly, they want straight talking not spin; they want to hear the proposition, and its pros and cons, clearly and without embellishment. The same goes for people working in organisations. In *Winning*, the latest book by Jack Welch, high profile ex-CEO of General Electric, lack of candour is described as the 'biggest dirty little secret in business'.

Ironically, the brand consultant might then point out that those who strive faithfully to model and espouse Christ out in the world, rather than take refuge within the confines of a special building or exclusive club, *reinforce* at least two basic lessons for aspiring secular marketers: 1) a quality brand is authentic, enduring, consistent, and meets the contemporary customer's need; and 2) seasoned influential customers reject the emotional pull of the 'affluenza' of consumerism; they realise that there is more to life and their identity than the brands they buy.

Finally, he might even point out that, if the Bible is to be the guide, a provocative brand like 'evangelical', or a friendly brand like 'liberal', are as unnecessary and misleading as Catholic, Protestant, Anglican, or whatever. Biblically there is only one genuine church, comprising genuine followers of Christ who will naturally want to share the Truth with passion and rigour, albeit in a Christlike manner. Nevertheless, as for any global or universally applicable 'brand', it is eminently advisable to reflect in its presentation the idiom of each 'market segment'; but never at the expense of its 'core values'.

Is that the kind of church you might be interested in, or would you rather stay with the conventional wisdom that says any kind of church is for the birds?

Stay with the conventional wisdom

Have you ever thought deeply about the directions our pluralist, tolerant post-modern world might be taking us? If we eliminate God from the equation, the door is wide open for other highly influential leaders and thinkers to sway conventional wisdom. Earlier I referred to Hugh Mackay's book; here are two other examples of the countless attempts to impact current debate, without God.

I have just read a review in *The Age* newspaper of *The Immortality of Goodness*, written by highly respected, retired Australian businessman and politician, John Siddons. I sympathise with Siddons, because he has taken four years to write his book about 'a complete system of morality that is independent of religion, race and culture', and hopes it will help teach ethics to children and young people – a laudable objective because 'young people used to learn basic ethics in church, but there is no religion in schools. Even morality is taboo'. He concludes that 'we need a precept of morality based on human rationality, not religion'.

Apparently he draws heavily on the *nonconsequentialist* moral theory proposed in *The Theory of Morality*, written by his Australian friend and philosopher, Alan Donagan. Before he died prematurely in 1991, Donagan was Professor of Philosophy at both Chicago University and the California Institute of Technology. He systematised traditional Hebrew-Christian morality to deal with contemporary issues, and was deeply influenced by Kant. Although I cannot comment on Siddons' conclusions because I have not read his book, I mention it as an example of someone genuinely attempting to meet the secular world on its terms, but without the anchor of any transcendent source of morality, and hence any allowance for our supposed predicament before God.

Atheist Peter Singer, the Australian Professor of Bioethics at Princeton University's Center for Human Values, is another kind of rationalist, who says: 'My work is based on the assumption that clarity and consistency in our moral thinking is likely, in the long run, to lead us to hold better views on ethical issues.'

Probably the world's most prominent contemporary philosopher, his proposed alternative, known as *preference utilitarianism*, replaces the 'sanctity of life' ethic with 'quality of life'.

The aim is to maximise the preferences or choices of the greatest number of persons and minimise the pain of all feeling creatures. But he confines his definition of *persons* to those who are self-aware and so have *interests and preferences* (like living or dying), thus creating a new category that excludes some humans and includes some intelligent animals. Hence his radical views on infanticide (a newborn child is not self-aware so has no interests or preferences concerning living or dying), abortion, euthanasia, animal rights, and even bestiality – deeply disturbing issues that you and I may have to confront, sooner or later.

This raises a key distinction in the focus of our decision-making between *actions*, their *consequences*, and their *causes*. Let's start with those who focus on consequences. According to people like Singer, actions are not wrong in themselves, but only in terms of their results. The beguiling school of thought, labelled *consequentialism*, has inherent risks, and to be consistent, its adherents must consider *its* consequences, four examples of which I list below.

First, we are confronted with the question of whether the end ever justifies the means. Mackay for one warns that this is 'one of the most seductive of all moral arguments', a slippery slope wisely avoided.

Second, we have the difficulty of fully assessing the potential outcomes of actions. Like the effect of the butterfly on weather patterns, how can we confidently predict the reverberating and lasting impact of any spoken word or action? For instance, how can parents objectively weigh the consequences of trying to improve a desperately unhappy marriage against the effect of divorce on the children? International research shows that, despite long-lasting painful memories, most children of divorced parents – 75 to 80 percent – do not suffer major psychological problems. On the other hand, this leaves a mere 20 to 25 percent permanently scarred. Of course unhappy marriages cause unhappy children too. This is just one example of how dangerous statistics can be in the hands of the utilitarian who attempts to measure the greatest good for the greatest number.

Third, the level of agreement about what is right and wrong appears directly proportional to the assessment of the seriousness of the offence. This leads to inconsistencies, critical legal issues and misuse of scientific findings. For instance, most readily agree that Hitler, Stalin and bin Laden committed monstrous crimes, but there is unease surrounding other topical issues, including those to do with life and death (e.g. abortion, embryonic stem cell extraction and euthanasia) and sexual union outside heterosexual marriage (e.g. co-habitation, promiscuity and homosexual activity).

Fourth, who creates the rules and who enforces them? Humanist Max Hocutt, who denies God's existence and consequently admits there is no moral law, has stated in *Toward an Ethic of Mutual Accommodation*: '… if there were a morality written up in the sky somewhere but no God to enforce it, I see no reason why we should obey it. Human beings may, and do, make up their own rules.' I don't know whether Darwin was lamenting or asserting when he wrote:

A man who has no assured and ever present belief in the existence of a personal God or of a future existence with retribution and reward, can have for his rule of life, as far as I can see, only to follow those impulses and instincts which are the strongest or which seem to him the best ones.

Darwin seems to be implying that humankind is either distinguished by a sense of God-given morality, or he is just another beast. So do humanists, who view people trying to adhere to God's law as sick and repressed, also consider rape to be a sickness, when other beasts rely on their strength to propagate?

This leads us to those who focus on causes. Frequently arguments are advanced to excuse certain behaviour on yet to be proven genetic or psychological grounds: 'How responsible am I for my actions?' Some allow homosexuality, because they believe it to be biologically determined, but would not condone paedophilia and incest, despite speculation that they too could be gene based. Neither would they defend bin Laden on the grounds of 'diminished responsibility'.

The plea of diminished responsibility based on psychological theories could eventually lead to the disintegration of a rational legal system, because without a comprehensive moral law to discern 'rights' from 'wrongs', how do we decide who is mentally ill or 'sick'? Steve Jones, Professor of Genetics at University College London, tackles this vexing question in his book *In the Blood: God, Genes and Destiny*. He concludes that:

> Although free will is constrained for many people because of the genes they carry, their actions must be treated as intentional simply because good order demands it … Society is not a product of genes but of people, and what they do must be judged by the law and not by science.

Science is a moving feast, and newly emerging fields require close examination. For instance, recently an article in *The Lancet*, the world's top medical journal, called bioethics a 'bankrupt' discipline. Prof Roger Cooter, of University College London, is not alone in his assessment that 'hardly wet behind the ears, bioethics seems destined for a short lifespan'.

It is also interesting to note that, just as biological determinism gathers steam, it might already be superseded by another view:

human behaviour is actually the product of complex *interaction* between our genetic makeup and environment. Acclaimed science writer Matt Ridley forcefully argues that our 'natures emerge via nurture'. Yet it may be different for personality development, as touched on earlier.

Ultimately *ideas* are the primary cause of actions and their consequences, but in evaluating an idea, we must always go back to *its* source and intent. Then we can avoid being misled by what subsequent followers might or might not choose to do with it; we ignore the lessons of history at our peril.

Karl Marx wrote in 1861: 'Darwin's book is very important and serves me as a basis in natural selection for the class struggle in history.' Now look at the consequences of this idea being adopted *en masse*. Followers of Marx proceeded to enslave two billion men and women politically, and their evolutionary ideology resulted in an estimated 110 million lives lost in the Soviet Union, 30 million in China, and countless others around the world, not to mention the unspeakable deprivation and humiliation endured by many who survived.

Hitler found in evolution his knockout weapon against Christianity, which he vilified as 'the most fatal, seductive lie that ever existed'. In *Mein Kampf* he wrote: 'I do not see why man should not be just as cruel as nature ... all that is not of pure race in this world is trash.' If you consider yourself to be an atheist, you might be interested to know that Hitler's sage and hero was Friedrich Nietzsche, probably the most articulate and influential spokesman for modern atheism, who said in his *Antichrist*: 'I call Christianity the one great curse, the one enormous and innermost perversion, the one great instinct of revenge, for which no means are too venomous, too underhand, too underground, and too petty.'

I hasten to add that all atheistic evolutionists and humanists who extend their thinking into the ethics domain need not be in sympathy with Nietzsche, but are you prepared to be advised by them, on what you ought or ought not do, when history suggests that a 'moral society' without a transcendent God does not fare too well? Of course it appears reasonable to draw parallels between the ravages of Marxisim and Nazism and the deplorable record of the Christian church down through the ages.

However there is a marked difference, and it lies between the sources and intent of the two ideas, not their wilful interpretation. In contrast to Darwin *et al*, at the heart of Christ's teaching is the assertion that life is sacred – we are infinitely valuable, created by God in his image to know him – and far from 'dancing to the DNA', we have to act according to God's law of love, love both for him and for our neighbour, as spelt out in the Ten Commandments. According to the Bible, God then looks after the consequences: 'And we know that in all things God works for the good of those who love him …' (Romans 8: 28).

For many contemporary intellectuals, the ideas of God and sheer holiness are simply *passé*. Atheists assert that humans have created God as a crutch, to fulfil a psychological need to cope with all that nature and life throw at us. In *The Natural History of Religion*, Hume argued that 'the primary religion of mankind arises from anxious fear of future events'. This form of religion in primitive cultures is known as animism, where people attribute personal gods to inanimate things, particularly threatening natural forces like thunder and fire. They can then try to appease the gods' anger through various practices like sacrifice.

But have you wondered why anyone would create a *holy* God, a God that cannot be manipulated? Apparently Christ's disciples were terrified out in the boat, but instead of becoming calm when he quieted the storm they were much more afraid, because they had encountered the awesome power of a holy God. English playwright Tom Stoppard puts the crutch on the other foot; he says that atheism is the crutch for all those who cannot bear the reality of God. With guilt comes denial; one could argue that the atheist has an equal psychological need to deny God, because then he doesn't have to be morally accountable to this supreme holy being. Of course the existence of God cannot be proved by our psychological need to create or deny him.

Humanists continue to work towards developing their idea, a science of ethics based on atheism and evolution, and in the process disregard and disparage the ideas that 1) a supreme God might attach grave significance to the actions we take, and 2) he alone is in a position to deal with the countless consequences. What do you make of these differing perspectives? Paul Kurtz, author of the *Humanist Manifesto II*, states:

> The traditional super-naturalistic moral commandments are especially repressive of our human needs. They are immoral insofar as they foster illusions about human destiny (heaven) and suppress vital inclinations.

Chesterton comes to the opposite conclusion for those who follow Christ (which to be fair differs markedly from the thousands of instructions spelt out for the Muslim):

> ... the curtness of the Ten Commandments is an evidence, not of the gloom and narrowness of a religion, but, on the contrary, of its liberality and humanity. It is shorter to state the things forbidden than the things permitted: precisely because most things are permitted, and only a few things are forbidden.

An example of one such forbidden action is divorce, unless the other party commits adultery, which is also forbidden. The complex proposed changes to how child maintenance payments should be calculated in Australia is just one instance of the mess we create for ourselves when we focus on the consequences rather than the action. To the long-suffering taxpayer with a spouse and children, this lengthy quote from *The Age* editorial says it all:

Research by the Australian Institute of Family Studies found that almost two-thirds of divorced fathers believed the present system of maintenance payments was not working, while three-quarters said it was unfair. At the same time, half of single mothers also believed the scheme did not work and was unfair. This level of dissatisfaction can hardly be in the interests of separated parents or their children and speaks of a system in need of reform. A taskforce headed by Sydney University law professor Patrick Parkinson has responded by proposing new guidelines for determining child support. It has calculated the costs of raising children and proposes a cap on payments so that the money cannot be used to maintain a former spouse. The system also takes account of the earnings of both parents and the amount of time children spend in the care of each parent. It will mean the amount a father pays will be reduced if the children spend one night a week or more at his house. The proposals also take into account the likelihood of a non-resident parent starting a new family. It allows divorced fathers to quarantine earnings from a second job or overtime from their maintenance assessment – but only if these earnings began after separation. More controversially, a divorced father who remarries and has a new child will be able to deduct the cost of that child from his assessable income before his maintenance payments are calculated.

Professor Parkinson concedes the proposals may result in many resident parents (mostly mothers) receiving less child support, and the recommendations have been criticised on these grounds. On the other hand, it is also recommended that the Child Support Agency be given more power to investigate the wealth of the non-custodial parent. Under the proposals, resident parents will also keep the family tax benefit (unless fathers have the children for more than 35 per cent of the time).

Consequences! God's provision of a simple set of laws, as spelt out in the Bible, obviates the need to be immersed in this kind of treacle. It also obviates the need to struggle with the implementation of new rules advanced by people like Singer.

Gordon Preece, former director of the Centre for Applied Christian Ethics at Ridley College in Australia, (currently Director and Dean at Macquarie Christian Studies Institute, Macquarie University), observes that 'underneath his seemingly benign agenda lies perhaps the most radical challenge to Christian ethics proposed in recent times'. In the book, *Rethinking Peter Singer*, Preece and three of his scholarly colleagues critique Singer's views in a rigorous manner. One of their most penetrating observations is that Singer tends to *caricature* Christ's teaching and the biblical account of creation. They give a number of instances of Singer's disproportionate emphasis of certain aspects, omission of key elements, and linking biblical teaching with people or events that, by association, damn the Scriptures.

According to Preece, Singer 'consistently fails to place a text in its immediate context, then in its argument, then in its book, then in the canon ... Singer systematically misuses the biblical evidence through tendentious citation'. This lack of balance should not be expected from anyone rated as a great thinker. Yet Preece also warns that many Christian readers of the Bible fall into the same trap. When a wealthy Westerner excuses the poverty gap in biblical terms with the quote: 'There will always be poor people in the land', he or she conveniently overlooks the second part of the very same verse: 'Therefore I command you to be openhanded toward your brothers and toward the poor and needy in your land' (Deuteronomy 15: 11), and in the process sidelines the overall thrust of the Bible. Take just one other quote: 'He who oppresses the poor shows contempt for their Maker, but whoever is kind to the needy honours God' (Proverbs 14: 31).

Although Christ commanded us to love a God that many say does not exist, he also commanded us to love our neighbour, whom we do know exists. Numerous people have their own ideas about who our neighbours are and how we should deal with them. Singer espouses a strong moral concern, and appears to have worked out what is best, yet is selective in determining the beneficiaries.

In our global, poverty-stricken world, who do you think is our neighbour, and how much do you give to the marginalised? How do you view the attitude of our affluent, secular West to the shocking plight of millions suffering hunger, loneliness, illness and disability? Last night I watched a television report about desperate Sudanese children, the innocent victims of systematic and brutal ethnic cleansing. The heart-rending footage was immediately followed by three commercials, the first for a pretty ordinary $1,499 diamond ring, followed by a hi-tech television and a gourmet pet food product, featuring a big, healthy, very well fed dog. You might be interested to know that Australians spend $2.2 billion a year on their pets compared with $2.0 billion on foreign aid.

Someone once said that the measure of generosity is not how much we decide to give but how much we keep. Another said it is the function of how much it costs the giver in relation to the degree of unworthiness of the recipient, pointing to Christ as the ultimate exemplar, because he supposedly gave all for those who despised him. A wise friend of mine goes even further when he says that to be truly Christ-like we must not only share our material blessings at arm's length, but also 'walk alongside' those in need. Even as the money pours into the tsunami-stricken region it is still reasonable to ask how we really measure up against these demanding criteria.

At the root of the poverty scandal, and other severe practical issues like efficiency of distribution, etc, is greed; and there are two guilty parties, the 'have lots', and the corrupt, brutal regimes dominating the 'have nots'. When we personally encounter such injustice we are tempted to shout at God about his apparent disinterest; but perhaps through this very poverty he is shouting at us. Individuals and institutions need a fundamental change of heart. But in the big scheme of things, what can I do to make a difference? Nothing will happen unless each of us starts by simultaneously standing up against the institutions and dealing with our own self-centredness.

Perversely, self-centredness seems to be the main focus of the aforementioned New Age quest for spiritual answers.

Wrap up

On re-reading this chapter there are three seemingly interdependent themes worth reinforcing – self-centredness, guilt and arrogance.

Liberals and New Agers talk much about realising our potential. MacLaine's preoccupation with self – the philosophical term being 'solipsism' – resonates with Spong's New Reformation and the mantra of many psychologists. This fixation is what the so-called rebellion of humanity is all about, an obvious anathema to such proponents of self-help theories.

According to Stott, New Agers are motivated by a laudable threefold aspiration – the quest for 'transcendence, significance, and community'; he argues, however, that they are looking in the wrong place. Christ was also very big on realising our potential, and paradoxically demonstrated that the only way up is down:

we discover ourselves when we lose ourselves. Discovering self is a by-product of denying self, i.e. putting God and our neighbour first. It is important to note that he distinguished between a corrupt self-love, and the self-love that has a due regard for the dignity of our nature made in the image of God, and a due concern for the welfare of our soul and body.

Like the New Agers, many liberals put a lot of emphasis on psychology, and psychologists say the biggest problem today is unresolved guilt. Both schools reject the idea of guilt 'as a motivator of behaviour', thus choosing to discredit the notion of man's predicament before God and the unique role of Christ. Sproul thinks differently about the matter, aligning guilt with an analogy of physical pain. Just as pain is a vital signal that a part of our body requires remedial attention, we *know* that the only antidote for guilt is forgiveness, not denial. In order to receive the antidote, the Bible says we first need to be made aware of our sin. We can then rely on God's forgiveness to free us from the paralysis of guilt, and allow us to power on in his calling.

Thinking about guilt and forgiveness brings to mind the 'grieving process', which I use (with a light touch, in deference to the psychologists) to help business teams decide how to extricate themselves when they are up against 'the wall'. Simplistically, our version suggests there are five natural steps to be worked through before we can move on – denial, anger, bargaining, acceptance, and 'letting go'. We have all experienced this painful course, and know the difficulty of trying to accelerate our progression, especially at the personal level.

Like 'alternative' healing practices, forgiveness is becoming a topic for scientific investigation. For example, early indications in HIV/AIDS patients suggest that forgiving those the patients blame lowers stress hormones, which in turn affects the immune system. Lydia Temoshok, director of the Behavioural Medicine Program at the University of Maryland, says 'It's letting go, *and* I forgive you. It's something about that added component. Then you close the circle. It's not just stopping something, but starting a new pattern'.

I can vouch for that. A friend of mine once went behind my back on a business deal. For months the hurt smouldered, and it was unbearable. One day, in desperation I blurted out that I wanted to forgive him and say no more. The resultant transformation in both of us, not to mention our relationship, was remarkable. I only wish I had had the courage and humility to do the same thing in a number of other instances earlier in my life.

Interestingly, when I have observed people subconsciously or unconsciously follow this approach for self-inflicted guilt, more often than not they simply cannot *will* themselves to let go – 'I still feel guilty'. It is worth noting that in God's sight we are either morally guilty or not guilty, regardless of how we feel. Sproul highlights this important distinction between *being* guilty and *feeling* guilty. Although the latter tends to follow the former, we all know of instances where one exists in the absence of the other.

The Bible warns that this is fertile ground for Satan, again rejected by liberals and New Agers, but depicted in the Bible as an invisible reality, immeasurably more dangerous and deceptive than banal caricatures. A literal meaning for the word Satan is 'accuser', because Satan not only tempts but also accuses, thus amplifying our feeling of remorse when we are guilty, and making us feel guilty when we are innocent or when we have already been forgiven by God. Sproul calls him a 'skeleton rattler'. In contrast, when God convicts us of our sin He assures us of His forgiveness at the same time.

This appears to be a much more powerful remedy than a psychologist's rationalisation of guilt, counselling that we simply have to overcome being victimised by some Victorian taboo, so that we can 'empower ourselves to realise our potential'. By the way, please don't think that I am of the school that believes all psychologists should be shot. Nevertheless I do believe that no psychologist is sufficiently super-human to block out completely his or her own preferences and so deal with troubled clients in an absolutely neutral fashion.

Now for a final word on the apparent arrogance shown by many contemporary thinkers. Sir Julian Huxley was one of the most influential evolutionists in the twentieth century. For him, the human race was evolving upwards and our duty was to aid the process by 'improving' the human stock. He believed physical and mental abilities were caused much more by hereditary than environmental and conditioning factors. Several extracts of Huxley's *The Stream of Life* indicate the potential consequences of these ideas:

> We ought to try to ensure that the children who are to come into the world shall have the best possible constitution; and this can be done by some control of the individual's right to bring children into the world … Reproduction can be stopped by segregating defectives in special institutions, or by artificial sterilization – an operation that is trifling for men, though rather more serious for women, while the psychological effects, again especially in men, are negligible … What is one to think of the misplaced kindness which, to give an actual recent case, takes an epileptic woman to hospital to be operated on to remedy sterility; or the sentimentality which rejoices at the 'happiness', so called, generated by the marriage of two deaf mutes? … Let us not forget that we men are the trustees of evolution, and that to refuse to face this problem is to betray the trust put into our hands by the powers of the universe.

Huxley was a respectable, highly educated Englishman who held prestigious positions in his career. Today his ideas are cloaked in the respectable garb of modern medicine, and many modern humanists continue to risk coming across as intellectual snobs. Frequently Huxley referred to the 'feeble-minded', implying that only the 'intelligent' are fit to determine right and wrong. Stephen Hawking would not have even survived in the science fiction classic *Brave New World*, written by novelist Aldous Huxley, who held views similar to those of his brother Sir Julian. But before we dismiss Huxley eugenics as extremist, remember the millions of babies aborted today because of disability or inconvenience, and the possibility of manipulating DNA, even down to preferred eye colour.

Another Australian bioethicist, Julian Savulescu, Professor of Applied Ethics at Oxford, tells parents they have a *moral* obligation to genetically modify their children. He insists that this is not Nazi eugenics, because Nazi eugenics was 'a state-imposed vision'. But eugenics is eugenics, including Savulescu's free-market, libertarian version, which we know is a more effective way to change public preferences than by dictate.

People like Savulescu and Singer enjoy wide media coverage because they seem to court controversy, and they gain *gravitas* because of their perceived credentials as leading academics from august institutions. Most of us find the intellectual horsepower of such thinkers extremely daunting, but perhaps it is reassuring that a big brain is not a requirement to qualify for jury service or parenting. As a mere punter, what is your verdict in regard to the shifting riptides of conventional wisdom? On what basis do you want your young children to learn how to make wise decisions?

CHAPTER NINE

THREE TESTS

A critical evaluation

Having stayed in the helicopter, now is the time to apply your mind and heart to my overall line of argument and the proposed alternatives, using the three tests mentioned at the outset, much of which I owe to Sproul: *Is it rational? Is it real? How certain can I be?* Only after we undergo this process can we put our *faith* in something.

The painstaking nature of rigorously evaluating competing arguments became very real to me on two separate occasions in the courtroom. Years ago I found myself locked away with eleven other jurors in Melbourne, deciding the fate of a man charged with culpable driving after allegedly causing the tragic death of two young children. Both opposing barristers eloquently argued their respective cases for many days, and when the twelve of us retired to consider our verdict, someone said with a sigh of relief that it would not take us long to decide that the man was guilty. As most readily nodded in agreement, I felt very uncomfortable muttering that I was not so certain that it was beyond reasonable doubt.

All of us were pretty ordinary people, and I suspect not one had ever been challenged to undergo such a rigorous decision-making process, involving a dispassionate examination of witness testimonies, evidence and clever argument, and divorced as much as humanly possible from any emotional feeling for the heartbroken family and friends of the victims. Nonetheless, it was immensely heartening how seriously we all then embarked on this rational process, and it took two days of intense deliberation before we reached a unanimous verdict.

The case seemed to hinge on the agonising legal question of what point in time did an offence occur. We delivered a 'not guilty' verdict on the grounds that the defendant had blacked out moments prior to the crash and was incapable rather than culpable. But why did an offence not occur when he consumed a dangerous cocktail of vodka and medication earlier that morning, as he had done for years? Or when he started to drink excessively at some earlier stage in his life? Or when something else happened to him or was done by him even earlier? Several times we went back to the judge with what we considered legal points requiring clarification, frustrated each time by being told 'that is for the jury to decide'.

Our verdict in this high profile case was predictably met with fury by the media and society at large, including my family and friends, stunned by how stupid a jury could be. I could only take solace in the thought that, without immersing themselves in the full process, other ordinary people just like us could not appreciate how demanding the notion of guilt beyond reasonable doubt can be. As the old Native American saying goes, 'never judge a man till you've walked a mile in his moccasins'.

On the second occasion, I was a very involved observer at the Old Bailey trial of a man charged with attempted murder. Eleven years ago, my beloved wife, Dorrie, sustained near fatal damage by being bashed over the head with a baseball bat in a London supermarket car park, from which she has thankfully made a remarkable recovery after her titanic struggle of several years. She valiantly continues to endure the frustration of short-term memory loss and chronic pain of a damaged neck and ringing ear. In this case the defendant was found guilty. The media and world at large hailed the verdict as the only rightful outcome, and although the evidence and arguments were overwhelming, I felt strangely relieved that the justice system had still been rigorously applied by a wise judge and troubled ordinary members of the jury.

I was interested to read an article by *Financial Times* columnist, Lucy Kellaway, after she had sat on a jury. She concluded that jury service would be a helpful experience for business teams. The twelve members did not know each other, underwent no 'trust exercises', and yet were the perfect team. Why? Because they were doing something important, i.e. deciding whether someone should go to jail; everyone tried to do a good job, everyone knew exactly what they had to do and were fully responsible, or 'empowered', they really listened to each other, and were respected and looked after. As for me, it was a 'humbling' and 'uplifting' experience for Kellaway.

So, unless you have a better idea, join the jury and apply the following three tests to my arguments, and the proposed alternatives, with all the rigour you can muster.

Is it rational?

To reach the conclusion that, because all chickens come from eggs, this chicken must have come from an egg, requires a purely abstract mental process using *deduction* – the logical approach that starts with the general and moves to the particular.

There are two universal principles that we use to test our logic: 1) there can be no contradictions, and 2) every effect must have a cause. You will probably think these are statements of the obvious; for example, to the surfer, the fin of a cruising shark cannot be and not be there at the same time! But such a precise definition of the law of non-contradiction is crucial. It allows you to distinguish properly between the word contradiction and two others frequently misused as synonyms – paradox, something that appears contradictory but under closer scrutiny is not, and mystery, something that we don't understand but is not therefore necessarily false.

RATIONALITY TEST

The law of non-contradiction

'Something cannot *be* what it is and *not be* what it is at the same time and in the same sense.' This statement does not mean that an egg cannot be both brown and oval at the same time; it just cannot be oval and not oval at the same time.

The law of causality

'Every effect has a cause.' This statement is true by definition, and is a corollary of the law of non-contradiction because, if that law is true, the law of causality must also be true.

Having hiccupped on this dose of abstract thinking, I can now hear you echoing modern teenage colloquialisms, 'whatever', and let's 'get real'. To restrict our approach to sheer rationality keeps us stuck in the mind, unable to move out into the real world.

Is it real?

To reach the conclusion that all chickens come from eggs requires an 'empirical' process using *induction* – the scientific approach based on experiment, observation and data collection.

But, in contrast to the logical approach, any such conclusion can only be based on probabilities. All we can say is that the probability quotient rises as we count more and more chickens from eggs. Because we will never be able to check the birth of every chicken, past, present and future, there will always be a chance that our conclusion is mistaken.

This introduces another well-accepted principle, or test, for sound thinking, which assumes that we can trust our senses of seeing, hearing, touching, smelling and tasting physical things, albeit with a touch of caution.

> ### REALITY TEST
> 'Sense perception is basically reliable.' This statement does not use the term *infallible* reliability, because we know that our senses are prone to distortion and error.

After being the driver in a serious car accident many years ago, I was amazed to hear three different versions of the incident from the three passengers, including the make and colour of the offending vehicle. Understandably, our observations were blurred by shock and the speed of the event. You may know the old adage that there are three versions for every lecture – what the speaker thinks he said, what the audience think they heard, and the words actually spoken. You will know the pain of misinterpreting another person's vibes.

But to conclude that *all experience is worthless* because we are sometimes mistaken seems irrational. In fact, more often than not, initial observations of physical things with the naked eye are confirmed, expanded and refined when we look more closely through the telescope or microscope. Also, we are often proved right when we back our intuition about non-physical things. We live by the 'reality test', even though it lacks the force of the first two principles.

Sproul points out that there are those who deny this principle with their lips, but not with their lives. John Cage, American avant-garde musician and mushroom expert, believed that everything is governed by random chance. To express this worldview he created crazy music by random chance, but when picking mushrooms, he avoided the poisonous ones. His working assumptions were that mushrooms can't be poisonous and non-poisonous at the same time, and that having eaten one he can't be dead and alive at the same time. He seemed to stake his music on irrationality and his life on rationality. He was *certain* in his admission that 'if I approached mushrooms in the spirit of my chance operation, I would die shortly'.

How certain can I be?

For each step in the thinking process we have to evaluate potential conclusions against the 'certainty test'. Even though the *Oxford Dictionary* definition for 'certainty' is 'undoubted fact', Sproul says we choose to apply it at three different levels, dependent on the situation: absolute certainty, feeling certain, and legal certainty.

CERTAINTY TEST

Absolutely certain

At the abstract level there can be no doubt. For example, a triangle has three sides.

Feeling certain

When we see, hear, touch, taste or smell something, we are extremely confident. For example, the surfer exits the water in great haste when he spots the cruising shark fin.

Legally certain

Comprehensive evidence must be gathered from eyewitnesses and technical experts, presented clearly and objectively, and then weighed up by an independent judge or jury who must decide: *is it beyond reasonable doubt?*

Because of the quantity and quality of information available, and the reliability of our senses to perceive, our degree of certainty will always rest on probabilities. This is the basis on which our legal system dispenses justice.

We put our *faith* in this system, trusting that it will deliver justice, even to the extent of deciding whether the accused live or die. But it must work with *reasonable*, not *incontrovertible* evidence, and allow for the limitations and liabilities of human error. An *Oxford Dictionary* definition of the word faith is 'belief founded on authority', and the original Greek word means 'persuasion'. This suggests that, far from being blind, real faith is in fact *reasoning trust*. Go back to the triangular depiction of faith; it equally applies in our contemporary decision-making at every level.

POSTSCRIPT

Time out

A few years ago at a luncheon in the City of London, I was fortunate enough to be amongst a number of leading business and other decision-makers who took time out to ponder some of the weighty issues of the day. Much wisdom was shared, but only two comments made a lasting impression on me: 'there is too much reaction and not enough reflection' and 'we have forgotten how to have fun'. Interestingly, both came from the then Bishop of London.

So I invite you to pause, take precious time out from the busyness of life and consider the argument set out in this book, premise by premise. Having stuck it out to the end, you may feel deeply challenged and begin to query some of the fundamental tenets ingrained in your approach to making decisions. Despite how you *feel*, I hope you will *think* this is a good thing.

In a hostile, messed up world, clear thinking requires us to consider seriously the distinction between ideas, the resultant actions, and the consequences. It starts by having the humility and courage to ask the right questions of the right people. Turning this around, what are some of the questions, and who are some of the people, you might prefer to *avoid* in your decision-making?

I said at the outset that I do not wish to impose my views, but to conclude it is probably only fair to spell out the basis for my decision-making at work and at home. After applying the rationality and reality tests to the line of argument under investigation, I am *certain beyond reasonable doubt* that there is an infinitely superior, *single* alternative to the prevailing conventional wisdom, and any other way I might like to concoct, because of three irresistible conclusions – there is a loving and holy God as revealed through creation, our hearts, biblical authors and Christ; Christ is as portrayed in the Bible; and the Bible is utterly trustworthy.

My predicament and the solution become self-evident, along with steady co-ordinates to guide my journey. In fact, my origin and destiny are fused into one anchor point – the God as finally revealed in the person of Christ. When I am confused about any decision, answers to the age-old questions of 'is it right?' or 'is it wise?' can usually be clarified by contemplating what Christ would decide in the situation or what would please God. Like the eye is to the body, the conscience is to the soul – designed to detect and discern God's enlightenment.

Similar to millions of others, my *experience* affirms the Bible's claim that the proof is finally in the eating: 'Do not conform any longer to the pattern of this world, but be transformed by *the renewing of your mind*. Then you will be able to test and approve what God's will is – his good, pleasing and perfect will' (Romans 12: 2).

On looking back over this text two intensely personal questions arise – how clear and committed am I to this profound call, and how effectively do I communicate my position to those around me?

Clarity and commitment

Perhaps my conclusions are startling for those who know that I am not easily persuaded and like to do it my way, yet there are some inescapable factors I am forced to face:

- Secularism, science *per se*, psychological analysis, man-made religions and other elaborate thought systems do not provide clear, coherent answers to some of the most important questions in public and personal life. Hence they cannot yield a sufficiently robust and comprehensive framework against which to make wise decisions.

    I have discovered that we can only comprehend the single alternative when we suspend all prejudice and hostility, open our minds, learn, and humbly accept that as mere mortals we can never expect complete answers to all our questions.

- I would prefer to be known as a follower of the Christ of the Bible, rather than a Christian, because of the diverse, negative and limited connotations the term Christianity evokes in many minds, either through prejudice or bad experience.

    Although critical of the institutional church, I must remain fully involved for three reasons: accessibility to the wisdom and support of other fellow travellers, the opportunity to contribute to the wider world through its auspices, and the chance to effect greater change from within.

- My walk with God has veered from exhilaration to despair, in the struggle to abide by God's law and uphold his requirement to be a good citizen, corporately and personally, even when it means taking a lone stand against the tide.

    Making some decisions can take time and courage. In my times of weakness I have often been sustained by the unstinting support and affirmation of thoughtful, generous and Christ-like people, and a dynamic contemporary local church, characterised by balance without ambiguity.

- I have deeply hurt others and have been deeply hurt, but being made in God's image, and being of inestimable value to him, mean that our dignity can withstand any assault.

    I also know that brutal honesty is required to admit when my mind, emotions and will are not consistent with God's intent, and only through God's grace will my integrity and relationships be restored. When I view our wilful rebellion against a holy God in the light of the cross, I can only tremble, seek forgiveness, and bow in gratitude, because perfect justice has been dealt with on our behalf.

• Some extremely serious questions, like why there is so much apparent ignorance, misplaced faith, and suffering, have to be put aside as God's business.

In grappling with why the Asian tsunami should happen, religion editor of *The Age*, Barney Zwartz, quotes theologian Nicholas Wolsterstorff, who lost a son in an accident:

> Suffering is down at the centre of things, deep down where the meaning is. Suffering is the meaning of our world. For Love is the meaning. And Love suffers. The tears of God are the meaning of history ... But mystery remains. Why isn't Love-without-suffering the meaning of things? Why does God endure His suffering? Why does He not at once relieve His agony by relieving ours?

Zwartz concludes: 'All I can say is, God alone knows – and that's enough.' I agree. Apart from a flash of anger at first seeing my wife in casualty, after she suffered a random assault, I shared with her an extraordinary peace and lack of desire for revenge as she bravely fought back. Neither of us could imagine being without the presence of God, yet I do ponder how the thousands who prayed for her life would have reacted had their prayers been answered in a different way.

With some difficulty I accept that such painful issues should not be allowed to interfere with the business God has assigned to us: living as he would have us do; caring for and enjoying others and his creation; reaching out to him through prayer and exploration of scripture and nature; and proclaiming and defending the Truth.

- In contrast to these unanswerable questions, I believe there is a stunningly simple and profound answer to my biggest question – the meaning of life: I exist 'because God wanted me to be'.

  From my experience, ultimate meaning or reality is found in relationships, not clinical academic debate. As with any human spirit, my relationship with the invisible God is person-like, but it is the only bond that cannot be destroyed by wrongdoing or death. Moreover, once established through accepting God's forgiveness, it becomes the blueprint for all other relationships, where love is elevated above self. The clear implication is that we can only enjoy God's unconditional forgiveness once we have forgiven others unconditionally – much easier said than done on our power alone.

- There is no greater privilege than to sit alongside the deathbed of one's nearest and dearest, and to share the most intimate moments imaginable.

  In the face of imminent death, some were serene and some were solemn, but none was swaggering. During his last days, my godly father, who truly celebrated life, said that dying is just another voyage where you wave goodbye, only to be greeted on the other side.

After reading all this, my hope is that you might appreciate how offensive it is for me to be labelled with loaded terms like narrow-minded, bigoted, arrogant, religious, bible-bashing, fundamentalist or creationist. You see, I did not set out to find some 'narrow way'; in fact, as a product of today's supposedly inclusive world, the reverse would be much more palatable. But if I conclude, only after critical analysis and real life experience, that Christ is speaking the truth when he claims he is the only way up the mountain, how can *I* be bigoted and arrogant? Such a serious accusation must be levelled at Christ himself, and there seems to be a dearth of people willing to throw the first stone. I do believe, however, that there are many ways to the foot of the mountain, one of which I have just tried to map out for you.

Like you, I have to make a commitment, deliberately or by default. We either put our faith in the conventional wisdom of the day (whether it be secularism or any other man-made religion or school of thought) or in the Christ of the Bible. If we opt for the latter, the Bible becomes the operating manual for the running and fulfilment of the creator's design. And to be a committed follower of Christ entails much more than just striving to be a decent person who makes wise decisions. We entrust him with our very 'salvation', and have to take a stand. With all the knowledge, reasoning and objectivity I can gather, complemented by my life's experience, it's a no-brainer.

Nevertheless, I only intend to pose questions for you to ponder; so, if you have concerns about Christ, here are my two final questions: are they *reasonable* doubts, and who determines *how much* evidence is reasonable?

Some people are naturally credulous while others are obstinate. If you are honestly sceptical, you must at least be sceptical about your scepticism to be rationally consistent. Although we will never come close to knowing all the answers, the Bible tells us God has made plain all we need to know, so that we will have no excuse. To make the Truth even more self-evident, the invisible God became visible in Christ, and countless followers show us the immensely practical benefits of Christ-like decision-making and living.

However, there is also a cost. Christ made clear, particularly through his example, the degree of humility and courage required to take up the challenge and endure the derision of a hostile world. He said: 'If anyone would come after me, he must deny himself and take up his cross and follow me' (Mark 8: 34), although he did also promise that 'you will find rest for your souls. For my yoke is easy and my burden is light' (Matthew 11: 29-30). This rings in my ears when dinner companions or work colleagues find a follower of an Eastern religion much more fascinating than a follower of Christ. Or when one of the latest fictional bestsellers, like *The Da Vinci Code*, is considered much more fun to discuss than the boring old Bible.

You may rightly fear that if you acknowledge God's existence and the authenticity of Christ, you will have to change the way you make decisions and live, doing things his way, not yours. Or like me in the Sydney surf, you may not have even realised that you are caught in the rip of beguiling conventional wisdom.

Communication

As I reflect on how effective my words, and much more importantly, my life might have been in communicating my faith to others over the years, I am overcome by a deep sense of shame. This is all the more compounded by the fact I have been in the communications business for most of my working life. I can only leave it to you to rate the preceding pages of this book against my three criteria for effective engagement, mentioned at the start as 'simplicity, mutual understanding, and constructive dialogue'.

To wrap up, I can't help but revert once more to my cultural roots, where crows fly backwards to keep the dust out of their eyes, and where, if people were any more laid back, they'd fall over – you can take the boy out of the bush but not the bush out of the boy.

One of my favourite television commercials, which admittedly I had a bit to do with, was produced years ago to promote an animal health remedy for Australian livestock. It offers some useful insights into how people, passionate to share their view of the world, of whatever persuasion, can effectively engage with those who see things differently.

To demonstrate empathy with the bush culture, the opening scenes showed leathery old stockmen and their eager dogs mustering and treating a big mob in the heat, dust and flies, backed by a laconic jingle:

When your average Aussie feels things are going OK
He doesn't have a lot to say
He's confident, casual
He doesn't jump and shout
He'll just say, things are going OK

The script concluded with a question to three farmers: 'I see you're using (Product X), how's it working out?' Each responded with the same phrase 'they reckon it works', with emphasis on a different word to cover all possible reactions!

These farmers had decided to *try* the product because neighbours, *whom they respected*, had already done so with success. Typically, we look to the example of others we trust, before deciding whether to give something a go. The previous pages are just thousands of dry monochrome words, which only come to life through the technicolour lives of those who have chosen 'to believe to see'. Surely 'the medium is the message', and Christ has to be the perfect medium with the perfect message. We have become resistant to the hard sell, where the message is only presented in the most alluring terms. In sharp contrast to the soft soap appeal of the self-serving options that have no strings attached, Christ put both sides of his message starkly: he promised more than anyone in history, and warned that the road would be far from smooth.

Good communicators know that people only listen when they have a 'want' or 'perceived need', and are provided with the opportunity to make a clear connection with the proposed solution. As Christ did for us, the above commercial simply held up the mirror to the target audience, in the hope that the viewer would decide that such an accurate depiction of his situation suggested the vendor might just understand him and his possible need.

And this was done with a lightness of touch and gentle humour. There is much around us that suggests God has a sense of humour. I think another bishop or archbishop once said there are times when we should be serious, but we should never be solemn in this crazy world. As with an advertising jingle, 'the melody adds the magic to the lyrics'.

Finally, this commercial ended with a question, not a statement. From my experience, wise people more often than not answer a question with another more insightful question, to take the dialogue to a higher level, and to help us make our own decisions. Today's generation doesn't like to be told; two thousand years ago Christ modelled this approach on many occasions.

If you want to read for yourself more about God, Christ and the Bible, there are libraries full of books to confuse you, many very helpful and many not so. Here are some suggestions from my experience. For starters, why not try the Bible? Like Tony Blair, if you wanted to know more about Islam you would take a proper look at the Koran. Naturally it is helpful to use a modern English translation, like the *New International Version*, preferably with accompanying notes, and in conjunction with an explanatory book, e.g. *What's in the Bible* by R C Sproul and Robert Wolgemuth.

Random dipping is not a good idea. As for any meaty tome, whether on subjects like politics, business management or parenting, you should first examine the structure and flow of the whole. Then you might read a chapter, the equivalent of a discreet 'book' in the Bible. If you become absorbed you will progressively read the other books in an order that seems most appropriate for you. A good start is the book of Mark, because it is relatively short and manageable, and clearly explains the identity, mission and call of Christ.

Alternatively, if you feel inspired to discuss the Bible in a group, find a church that is running a well-facilitated interactive Bible-based programme like *Christianity Explored*, which helps genuine enquirers explore the book of Mark, no holds barred (check the website www.christianityexplored.com).

For further reading about God and Christ you might even try *The Real Face of Atheism* by Ravi Zacharias, and *The Cross of Christ* by John R W Stott. By then you should have acquired the taste for more.

PERSONAL BACKGROUND

From the hush of the bush
to the crush of the push

Although I expect you will evaluate my line of argument on its merits, should you be interested, here is more of my personal story, which doubles as a heartfelt acknowledgements section, especially to those whose brave decisions have left a lasting legacy. My father used the above line to characterise my marriage to a blond city slicker from Sydney, and in a way it sums up my entire journey.

Around the mid 1800s two young Scots met in a small remote camp called Adelaide, having separately endured the dreadful sea journey half way around the world. They possessed nothing but a vague dream of better things in the new colony of Australia. They married, produced twelve children in quick succession, two of which died as babies, and eventually travelled many miles to the harsh hinterland and settled on virgin land near the Murray River.

Legend has it that this canny Scot chose the most heavily timbered country, where there was less grass than on the open plains, because he figured that the best ground was where the trees grew strongest. He then devoted his life to the back-breaking task of clearing big thirsty, tough river red gums. In subsequent droughts, neighbours came to him for water. This deep sense of custodianship of the land has been passed down through the generations, along with a simple, profound faith in Christ.

In fact, my great grandfather travelled many miles to select and cart the timber required to build one of Australia's first country churches, which still stands today in the corner of an isolated paddock. My grandparents and parents inherited the fruits of my great grandparents' labour, and faithfully tried to leave the farm in ever better shape for the next generation. One of my father's enduring legacies resulted from his passion to plant and nurture hundreds of trees. This was my birthplace and home during childhood.

Legend also has it that when my great grandfather announced he had found the spot to build their lives in the middle of nowhere, my great grandmother burst into tears, and he said 'a great help to a man you would be'. She was an unsung hero of Australia's modern origins, like many pioneering women. The farm, near Gannawarra, was named 'Auchterless' after her birthplace, and her portrait is in my study.

In my study there is also a recent picture of a solitary grave in the Australian hinterland (near Wagragobilly on the Darbalara road!), where my maternal grandmother was buried at 36 years of age. She married a somewhat detached, scholarly Englishman, who had migrated to the raw Australian outback, with only the shirt on his back, to teach Aboriginal children. I fondly remember trying to reciprocate his birthday cards, hand-written in copperplate calligraphy, and our childhood visits to his last posting, my introduction to Australia's original rich heritage. At the tender age of eight, my mother assumed responsibility for her four younger siblings. I never heard her complain about those early years.

Like the other kids in the district, I was brought up to learn about our heritage, how to raise and handle livestock, work cattle dogs, ride horses and tractors, plough, sow and harvest crops, shoot, fish, watch out for deadly snakes and spiders, marvel at the wonders of the stars, new birth and death, and touch nature in its raw state. The farm was a family business, where dad, mum and the four kids pitched in, modestly celebrated good years, and tightened the belt following crippling droughts, fires and locust plagues. When I look back to compare my simple upbringing with that of my children, I realise the great benefits of being able to share in and learn from such things firsthand, beginning at an early age. By the by, as television had not invaded our neck of the woods, evenings were spent listening to the radio soap of the day and playing various musical intruments together; fortunately I was blessed with a musically gifted family!

As a young man I turned away from rural life to the urban world of commerce. Although there is much I missed, I have no regrets. I especially remember my father's dry, laid back humour, typical of the bush. To this day I recall his only advice when I went away to school in the big smoke: 'Don't get caught looking up at the tall buildings because you will give yourself away.' There has never been any risk of that because I always walk head down, eyes fastened on the ground two steps ahead, watching out for snakes. Fortuitiously, as I pace the pavements of cities this instinct proves beneficial for other reasons.

I also benefit from another thing my father occasionally muttered when we were trekking through the bush: 'I am not lost, it's just that I don't know where I am at the moment.' This sentiment has echoed many times down through the passage of time, because being lost in the rip of life is even more scary than being lost in the bush.

I treasure the diverse experiences of a bush upbringing, university, marriage, fatherhood and grand-fatherhood, life in Australia and the UK, and work in small and big business throughout the world. Predictably, three of my defining moments have comprised my initiation into manhood in my twenties, marked by my father's untimely death, marriage, babies and mortgages; the inevitable mid-life crisis in my forties, finding myself at the end of a ladder I assumed went endlessly upward; and now a timeout as I enter my sixties, to contemplate past lessons and the prospect of growing old.

As a young man I also formulated my own customised version of Christianity, and later on, my wife and I became disenchanted with several local churches. Through our hectic thirties we relegated the whole thing to the back seat. We then became proactive again, mainly for the sake of our children, and have since enjoyed a progressive re-discovery of the life and teaching of Jesus Christ. It has been our good fortune to attend two outstanding inner London churches and learn from some of today's leading theologians and Christian philosophers, most of whom my secular and Christian friends have never heard. However, our disenchantment with the institutional church is undiminished.

So there is nothing at all notorious or newsworthy about this writer when compared with everyone else that has lived on this Earth and suffered at the hands of others, even though deep down I have often felt uneasy about my comparatively soft ride. I have already mentioned one momentous family event, when my wife was brutally attacked. Much more recently, the wonderful young ex-fiancé of my elder daughter, Prue, was stabbed to death in a scam involving the sale of her engagement ring. Like her mother, Prue's resilient faith has been an inspiration, along with her courage and concern for the grieving family.

These events were devastating for everyone involved, but similar headlines constantly reverberate across the world, and most such stories never see the light of day. I hope you will conclude that these personal tragedies have not come to dominate the way I think and feel, other than evoke huge respect for another two fine women in my life.

I conclude with deep gratitude to those who have acted as invaluable sounding boards – especially Tom Gregg, currently exposing himself to constant danger with the UN in Afghanistan, and our youngest daughter, Edwina, another special young woman with a strong faith and inspiring sense of justice. Ween, who relishes the tough questions, has egged me on when this all seemed too hard. And whilst continuing her demanding PhD schedule, she has generously applied her skills to challenge the logic and polish the text, although of course, all errors are mine. Lastly, but not least, I thank Dorrie for her loving patient endurance as I continue to battle the rip.

SELECT BIBLIOGRAPHY

Albright, William F (1966) *New Horizons in Biblical Research* (London & NY: Oxford University Press)

Aly, Waleed 'The tortures of heritage,' *The Age Review* (14 May 2005)

Badaracco, Joseph L *et al* 'Best of HBR on Leadership: Stealth Leadership,' *HBR OnPoint Enhanced Edition* (Product No BHOL2)

Bagaric, Mirko & Julie Clarke 'Not Enough Official Torture in the World? The Circumstances in Which Torture Is Morally Justifiable,' *University of San Fransisco Law Review* 39:3 (July 2005)

Behe, Michael J (1998) *Darwin's Black Box: The Biochemical Challenge to Evolution* (Touchstone Books, Simon & Schuster)

Blackburn, Simon (1999) *Think* (Oxford: Oxford University Press)
——(2001) *Ethics: A Very Short Introduction* (Oxford: Oxford University Press)

The Body Shop Core Principles, accessed in June 2005 at <http://www.thebodyshopinternational.com/web/tbsgl/values_approach.jsp#ocp>

Bone, Pamela 'Disregard the gospel according to St Peter,' *The Age* (13 July 2004)

Boot, Joe (1999) *In Six Days: Why 50 Scientists Choose to Believe in Creation* (ed) John F Ashton (Sydney: New Holland Publishers)
——(2002) *A Time To Search* (Eastbourne: Kingsway Communications Ltd)

Brooks, Jim (1985) *Origins of Life* (Sydney: Lion)

Bukhārī, Muh?ammad ibn Ismaˉ`iˉl (1978) [810-870] *Shiˉh al-Bukhari* (trans) Muhammad Muhsin Khan & Muhammad Asad (New Delhi: Kitab Bhavan)

Capgemini UK, *The Business Decisiveness Report* in 'Is choice anxiety costing UK 'blue chip' business?' (PR1487, 16 August 2004) available at <http://www.simpsonftpr.ie/clients/Capgemini/Pressreleases/UKSurveytopexecs.htm>

Caspi, Avshalom *et al* 'Children's Behavioral Styles at Age 3 are Linked to Their Adult Personality Traits at Age 26,' *Journal of Personality* 71:4 (August 2003), 495 - 513

Chesterton, G K (1959) *Autobiography* (London: Arrow Books)

Collins, Robin, Interview with Strobel (2004) *The Case for a Creator* (Grand Rapids, Mich: Zondervan)

—— 'A Scientific Argument for the Existence of God: The Fine-Tuning Design Argument,' in Michael J Murray (ed) (1999) *Reason for the Hope Within* (Grand Rapids, Mich: Eerdmans)

Cooter, Roger 'Perspectives: Historical keywords: Bioethics,' *The Lancet* 364, No. 9447: 1749

The Corporation [videorecording]/a documentary by Mark Achbar, Jennifer Abbott & Joel Bakan (Australia: Madman Cinema, 2003)

Covey, Stephen, Interview with Helen Trinca 'Stephen Covey: kick the control habit,' *The Australian Financial Review* (21 September 2004)

Darwin, Charles [1859] (1998) *The Origin of Species* (UK: Wordsworth Editions)

Dawkins, Richard (1976) *The Selfish Gene* (Oxford: Oxford University Press)

de Botton, Alain (2004) *Status Anxiety* (London: Penguin Books)

Denton, Michael (1986) *Evolution: A Theory in Crisis* (Chevy Chase, Md: Adler & Adler) cited in Strobel (2004) *The Case for a Creator* (Grand Rapids, Mich: Zondervan)

Ellul, Jacques (1990) *The Subversion of Christianity* (Grand Rapids, Mich: Eerdmans)

Frankfurt, Harry (2005) *On Bullshit* (Princeton: Princeton University Press)

Frost, Michael & Alan Hirsch (2003) *The Shaping of Things to Come* (Peabody, Mass: Hendrickson Publishers)

Gitt, Werner (1997) *In the Beginning was Information* (trans) Jaap Kies (Bielefeld: Christliche Literatur)

Gladwell, Malcolm (2005) *Blink: the Power of Thinking without Thinking* (NY: Little Brown & Company, Time Warner Book Group)

Glueck, Nelson (1969) *Rivers in the Desert: History of the Negev* (Philadelphia: Jewish Publication Society of America)

Glynn, Patrick (1999) *God: The Evidence, the Reconciliation of Faith and Reason in a Post secular World* (Three Rivers Press)

Gonzalez, Guillermo & Jay Wesley Richards (2004) *The Privileged Planet* (Washington DC: Regnery)

Gould, Stephen Jay (1982) *Evolution Now: A Century after Darwin* (London: Macmillan)

Goward, Pru 'Back to birds and bees,' *The Sunday Age* (21 November 2004)

Guy, Roslyn 'Ponder this,' *The Age* (16 May 2005)

Haldane, J B S (1927) 'When I am Dead,' in *Possible Worlds and Other Essays* (London: Chatto & Winduw) cited in Strobel (2004) *The Case for a Creator* (Grand Rapids, Mich: Zondervan)

Hamilton, Clive & Richard Denniss (2005) *Affluenza: When too much is never enough* (Melbourne: Allen & Unwin)

Hawking, Stephen W (1988) *A Brief History of Time: from the big bang to black holes (*Toronto & NY: Bantam Books)

Heidegger, Martin [1927] (1996) *Being and Time: A translation of Sein & Zeit* (trans) Joan Stambaugh (NY: State University of New York Press)

Hocutt, Max (1980) 'Toward an Ethic of Mutual Accommodation,' in *Humanist Ethics* (ed) Morris B Storer (Buffalo, NY: Prometheus Books)

The Holy Bible, New International Version (1973, 1978, 1984) (International Bible Society. Used by permission Zondervan Bible Publishers)

Hopkins, Philip 'Philosophical Siddons takes high moral ground,' *The Age* (21 May 2005)

Hume, David [1757] (1976) *The Natural History of Religion* (ed) A Wayne Colver (Oxford: Clarendon Press)

Huxley, Julian (1926) *The Stream of Life* (London: Watts & Company)

Hywood, Gregory 'Election 2004: it's about the economy *and* values, stupid,' *The Age* (5 August 2004)

Jaggi, Rohit 'Work-related stress costs £7bn a year', *Financial Times* (2 November 2004)

Johnson, Steven (2005) *Everything Bad Is Good for You: How Today's Popular Culture Is Actually Making Us Smarter* (NY: Riverhead Books)

Jones, E Stanley (1927) *The Christ of the Indian road* (London: Hodder & Stoughton)

Jones, Steve (1996) *In the Blood: God, Genes and Destiny* (London: HarperCollins Publishers)

Kant, Immanuel (1929) *Critique of Pure Reason* (trans) Norman Kemp Smith (London: Macmillan)

Kay, John 'Guru with more than conventional wisdom,' *FT International* (13 August 2004), 23

Keenan, Tony cited in Green, Shane 'Schools get a lesson in values,' *The Age* (28 November 2004)

Kellaway, Lucy 'Executives should first sit on a jury, then on the board,' *Financial Times* (25 April 2005)

Knott Kim (1998) *Hinduism: A Very Short Introduction* (Oxford: Oxford University Press)

The Koran (2000) (trans) N J Dawood (London: Penguin Books)

Kosky, Lynne cited in Green, Shane 'Schools get a lesson in values,' *The Age* (28 November 2004)

Küppers, Bernd-Olaf (1990) *Information and the Origin of Life* (Cambridge, Mass: MIT Press)

Kurtz, Paul (1980) *Humanist Manifesto I & II* (Buffalo, NY: Prometheus Books)

Landsman, Gregory (1995) *The Balance of Beauty Explodes the Body Myth* (Melbourne: Hill of Content)

Lecky, W H E (1869) *The History of European Morals from Augustus to Charlemagne* (New York: D. Appleton & Company)

Lewis, C S (1947) *Miracles* (London: Fontana)

——(1970) *Mere Christianity* (London: Fontana)

——(1999) *The Abolition of Man* (London: HarperCollins)

Lubenow, Marvin (1992) *Bones of Contention* (Grand Rapids, Mich: Baker Books)

Market Access Consulting & Research (2003) *Christian Media Project Qualitative Research* (September 2003)

McCamish, Thornton 'Secularism is no moral vacuum,' *The Age* (18 November 2004)

McDonald, John F (1983) 'The Molecular Basis of Adaptation: A Critical Review of Relevant Ideas and Observations,' *Annual Review of Ecology and Systematics* 14:93

McFadyen, Warwick 'A pipedream about values,' *The Age* (3 December 2004)

McGillion, Chris (2005) *The Chosen Ones* (Sydney: Allen & Unwin)

McGrath, Alister (1988) *Understanding the Trinity* (Grand Rapids, Mich: Zondervan Publishing House, Academie Books)

Mackay, Hugh (2005) *Right & Wrong: how to decide for yourself* (Sydney: Hodder)

MacLaine, Shirley (1983) *Out On A Limb* (New York: Bantam Books)

McLuhan, Marshall (2001) *The medium is the massage: an inventory of effects* (Corte Madera, CA: Gingko Press)

Mayr, Ernst (1970) *Populations, species, and evolution; an abridgment of Animal species and evolution* (Cambridge, Mass: Belknap Press of Harvard University Press)

Milbank, John (1991) *Theology and Social Theory beyond Secular Reason* (Oxford, UK & Cambridge, Mass: Blackwell)

Miller, Stanley L 'A Production of Amino Acids Under Possible Primitive Earth Conditions,' *Science* 117, No. 3046 (1953), 528-529

——in Ankerberg, John & John Weldon (1998) *Darwin's Leap of Faith* (Eugene, Or: Harvest House Publishers)

Mowrer, O Hobart cited in a Zacharias audio recording available at Ravi Zacharias International Ministries, Norcross, Georgia <http://www.rzim.org>

Muggeridge, Malcolm in Ravi Zacharias 'The Exclusivity and Sufficiency of Jesus Christ' (talk delivered at Salt Lake City, Utah, 14 November 2004)

Neville, Richard cited in McMahon, Stephen 'Savvy iPodders make retailers work hard for a sale,' *The Age* (25 July 2005)

Nietzsche, Friedrich W (2000) *The Antichrist* (trans) Anthony M Ludovici (Amherst, NY: Prometheus Books)

O'Donoghue, Ted & Matthew Rabin 'The Economics of Immediate Gratification', Working Paper Series, University of California, Berkeley (August 1997)

Oldstone-Moore, Jennifer (2003) *Understanding Confucianism* (London: Duncan Baird Publishers)

Packer, J I (1973) *Knowing God* (London: Hodder & Stoughton)

Palmisano Samuel J, Interview with Paul Hemp & Thomas A Stewart, 'The HBR Interview: Leading Change When Business Is Good,' *Harvard Business Review* (December 2004: 21)

Penfield, Wilder (1975) *The Mystery of the Mind* (Princeton: Princeton University Press) cited in Strobel (2004) *The Case for a Creator* (Grand Rapids, Mich: Zondervan)

Petroski, Henry (1996) *Invention by Design* (Cambridge, Mass: Harvard University Press)

Polkinghorne, John 'The Address' at National Prayer Breakfast (Westminster, London: 18 November 1992)

Preece, Gordon (2002) *Rethinking Peter Singer: A Christian Critique* (Downers Grove, Illinois: InterVarsity Press)

Preskill, John 'Quantum Computation,' talk delivered at *17th International Conference on General Relativity and Gravitation*, (Dublin, Ireland: 18-23 July 2004)

Rahula, Walpola (1974) *What the Buddha Taught* (New York, NY: Grove Press)

Ramsay, William M (1915) *The bearing of recent discovery on the trustworthiness of the New Testament* (London & NY: Hodder & Stoughton)

Ratzinger, Joseph, Interview in *La Repubblica*, repeated in Johnston, Bruce & Jonathan Petre 'Secular forces 'pushing God to margins',' *The Telegraph* (20 November 2004)

Rees, Martin (2000) *Just Six Numbers: The Deep Forces that Shape the Universe* (New York: Basic)

Ridley, Matt (2003) *Nature Via Nurture: Genes, Experience and What Makes us Human* (New York, NY: HarperCollins)

Robinson, Martin (1997) *The Faith of the Unbeliever* (Crowborough, East Sussex: Monarch Publications)

Rosenthal, Stanley 'Introduction to Tao Te Ching,' accessed in March 2005 at <http://www.larsonsworld.com/tao_buddhism_zen/taoteching_intro_rosenthal.html>

Sandage, Allan 'A Scientist Reflects on Religious Belief' accessed in April 2005 at <http://www.leaderu.com/truth/1truth15.html>

Sartre, Jean Paul [1938] (1964) *Nausea* (trans) Lloyd Alexander (New York, NY: New Directions)

Schwartz, Barry (2004) *The Paradox of Choice: Why More is Less* (New York, NY: HarperCollins)

Searle, John 'Do Brains Make Minds?' on the television programme *Closer to Truth* (Show 204, October 2000)

——'What is Consciousness?' on the television programme *Closer to Truth* (Show 107, June 2000)

Shrimpton, Jan cited in 'Battling the bullies,' *The Age* (22 November 2004)

Sinclair, Amanda 'Endnote,' *BOSS: Financial Review magazine* (June 2004)

Smith, Wesley J 'Now They Want to Euthanize Children In the Netherlands,' *The Daily Standard* (13 September 2004)

Spillane, Robert 'If you're happy and you know it…,' *Sunday Life: The Sunday Age Magazine* (29 May 2005)

Spong, John Shelby 'A Call for a New Reformation', accessed in November 2004 at <http://www.dioceseofnewark.org/jsspong/reform.html>

Sproul RC (1982) *Reason to Believe* (Grand Rapids, Mich: Zondervan)

——(1995) *Faith Alone* (Grand Rapids, Mich: Baker Books)

——material from various audio recordings available at Ligonier Ministries <http://www.ligonier.org>

——with Wolgemuth, Robert (2000) *What's in the Bible* (Nashville, Tennessee: W Publishing Group)

Stern, Stefan 'Me, me, me is business books' new obsession,' *Financial Times* (11 December 2003)

Stott, John (1986) *The Cross of Christ* (Illinois: InterVarsity Press)
———material from various audio recordings available at All Souls Church, Langham Place, London <http://www.allsouls.org>

Strobel, Lee (2004) *The Case for a Creator* (Grand Rapids, Mich: Zondervan) (NB: All conversations with Strobel derive from *The Case for a Creator*.)

Sunderland, Luther D (1984) *Darwin's Enigma: Fossils and other Problems* (Santee, CA: Master Book Publishers)

Temoshok, Lydia cited in Elizabeth Large 'Don't forget … forgive,' *The Baltimore Sun* (11 January 2005)

Thaxton, Charles B, Walter L Bradley & Roger L Olsen (1984) *The Mystery of Life's Origin* (Dallas: Lewis & Stanley)

Time Magazine 'The People Who Influence Our Lives,' *Time Magazine* (18 April 2005)

Tisdall, Simon 'Brave talk but no action: Darfur gets a familiar response from the west,' *The Guardian* (3 August 2004)

Tyler, Christian 'Reconciliation between God and science,' *Financial Times* (11-12 September 1999)

Vincent, Frank, Interview with Shiel, Fergus 'Trials & Tribulations,' *The Age* (16 May 2005)

Volokh, Eugene (2003) 'The Mechanisms of the Slippery Slope,' *Harvard Law Review* 116: 1026

Wanser, Keith in Boot (1999) *In Six Days: Why 50 Scientists Choose to Believe in Creation* (ed) John F Ashton (Sydney: New Holland Publishers)

Ward, Glenn (1997) *Postmodernism* (London: Hodder & Stoughton)

Ward, Peter D (2000) *Rare Earth: Why complex life is uncommon in the universe* (New York: Copernicus)

Warner, Philip (1992) *The SAS* (London: Warner Books)

Welch, Jack (2005) *Winning* (NY: HarperBusiness)

Wells, Jonathan (2000) *Icons of Evolution* (Washington DC: Regnery)

Wilder-Smith A E (1981) *The Natural Sciences Know Nothing of Evolution* (San Diego: Master Books)

Wilson, Robert [1929] (2003) *A Scientific Investigation of the Old Testament* accessed in May 2005 at <http://www.pcanet.org/history/findingaids/wilson/siot.html>

Wink, Walter (1998) *The Powers That Be* (New York: Doubleday)

Wolpert, Lewis (1991) *The Triumph of the Embryo* (Oxford: Oxford University Press)

Yun, Brother with Paul Hattaway (2002) *The Heavenly Man* (London: Monarch Books)

Zacharias, Ravi (2004) *The Real Face of Atheism* (Grand Rapids, Mich: Baker Books)

——material from various audio recordings available at Ravi Zacharias International Ministries, Norcross, Georgia <http://www.rzim.org>